D0213721

LISTENING FOR THE TEXT

*Property of
Charles A. Owen Jr.
Medieval Studies Library*

THE MIDDLE AGES SERIES

General Editor

RUTH MAZO KARRAS
Temple University

Founding Editor

EDWARD PETERS
University of Pennsylvania

A complete list of the books in the series
is available from the publisher.

LISTENING FOR THE TEXT

ON THE USES OF THE PAST

Brian Stock

PENN

UNIVERSITY OF PENNSYLVANIA PRESS

PHILADELPHIA

FOR MARUJA

Originally published 1990 by The Johns Hopkins University Press
Copyright © 1990 The Johns Hopkins University Press
Paperback edition published 1996 by the University of Pennsylvania Press

All rights reserved

Printed in the United States of America on acid-free paper

10 9 8 7 6 5 4 3 2 1

Published by
University of Pennsylvania Press
Philadelphia, Pennsylvania 19104-6097

Library of Congress Cataloging-in-Publication Data

Stock, Brian.
Listening for the text : on the uses of the past / Brian Stock.
    p.   cm. — (Middle Ages series)
Includes bibliographical references and index.
ISBN 0-8122-1612-1 (pbk. : alk. paper)
    1. Historiography.   2. Semiotics.   3. Hermeneutics.   I. Title.
II. Series.
D13.S837   1997
907'.2—dc20   96-41321
                                                        CIP

CONTENTS

Contents

PREFACE

I am grateful to the University of Pennsylvania Press for the invitation to have this volume appear in its Middle Ages Series. I also owe a great debt to Ralph Cohen, the editor of *New Literary History*, who first published versions of some of these chapters. Few have done as much as he has for the advancement of critical discussion in our time.

Wolfgang Schluchter and Günther Roth kindly solicited my paper for the conference on Max Weber and the Christian Middle Ages held at the Reimers Foundation, Bad Homberg, in 1986. I add my gratitude to two senior Weberian scholars for helping to shape my outlook over the years. These are S. N. Eisenstadt and Reinhard Bendix, to whom I am much indebted for their writings and for listening to my ideas from time to time. I owe a similar acknowledgment to Jacob Neusner for arranging a National Endowment for the Humanities conference at Brown University, also in 1986, where there was an opportunity to test some of the hypotheses I had evolved for medieval religious life against the evidence of Jewish and Christian antiquity. I thank William Scott Green and Jonathan Z. Smith for their comments on that occasion, which aided me in my rethinking of the issues. For other invitations to give papers revised in this volume I warmly thank Pamela O. Long and Brigitte Cazelles. Nor should I omit the kindness of William Scott Green in helping to set up a general session of the American Academy of Religion devoted to "textual communities" in 1985.

The views expressed in these essays are my own. But I have profited from discussions with a number of historians over the years. My earliest debt is to the late Sir Moses Finley, and to the tradition of classical studies at Cambridge represented by F. M. Cornford. The friendship of Jacques Le Goff has been a continual source of support. I am equally grateful to Georges Duby, through whose beneficence I lectured on some of the themes of the Introduction at the Collège de France in 1987. I thank others as well: in Paris, Jean-Claude Schmitt; in Toronto, Ambrose Raftis, C.S.B.; and, wherever our paths have crossed, Natalie Zemon Davis.

My obligations to figures in other disciplines are also numerous. I am grateful to Clifford Geertz and Jerome Bruner for delightful conversations, with the latter in the company of Carol Feldman. I have had the privilege of exchanging ideas with Jack Goody since the early 1980s. A more distant debt, but one I am happy to mention, is to Walter Ong, whose work on orality remains fundamental. I am also among the many beneficiaries of Hayden White's studies in historiography. There are others who have acted as friends and advisors: they include R. Howard Bloch, Gerald Bond, Fergus Craik, James S. Duncan, Martin Krygier, Richard C. Martin, and David Olson. To these names I add those of younger researchers who have taught me much: Wanda Cizewski, Paul Dutton, Pauline Head, Thomas Head, Aviad Kleinberg, Richard Landes, Seth Lerer, Guy Lobrichon, John Magee, Helen Solterer, and Haijo Westra. I am grateful to Peter Dreyer for the care with which he has read my typescript, and for many helpful suggestions.

I benefited from a Connaught Senior Fellowship from the University of Toronto during the period in which many of these essays were written.

ACKNOWLEDGMENTS

Some of the material in this book first appeared in the following publications:

"The Middle Ages as Subject and Object: Romantic Attitudes and Academic Medievalism," *New Literary History* 5 (1973–74): 527–47.

"Literary Discourse and the Social Historian," *New Literary History* 8 (1976–77): 183–94.

"Medieval Literacy, Linguistic Theory, and Social Organization," *New Literary History* 16 (1984): 13–29.

"Rationality, Tradition, and the Scientific Outlook: Reflections on Max Weber and the Middle Ages," in *Science and Technology in Medieval Society*, ed. Pamela O. Long, Annals of the New York Academy of Sciences, vol. 441 (New York, 1985), pp. 7–19.

"History, Literature, and Medieval Textuality," in *Images of Power: Medieval History/Discourse/Literature*, ed. Kevin Brownlee and S. G. Nichols, Jr., Yale French Studies, no. 70 (New Haven, 1986), pp. 7–17.

"Language and Cultural History," *New Literary History* 18 (1986–87): 657–70.

"Schriftgebrauch und Rationalität im Mittelalter," in *Max Webers Sicht des okzidentalen Christentums: Interpretation und Kritik*, ed. Wolfgang Schluchter (Frankfurt, 1988), pp. 165–83.

The Introduction draws on a few paragraphs from the Symposium on Literacy, Reading, and Power, Whitney Humanities Center, Yale University, November 14, 1987, published in the *Yale Journal of Criticism* 2 (1988): 198–99.

ORALITY, LITERACY, AND THE SENSE OF THE PAST

I

Ours is largely an ahistorical world. And yet we take history very seriously. The more remote the past becomes, the more we seem to concern ourselves with understanding it. We are no longer linked to our ancestors through common material conditions. If earlier ages still have a hold on us, it is through our thoughts about them.

The essays in this volume are about a segment of the past that runs roughly from the end of antiquity to the thirteenth century. More generally, they are about recollecting the past by putting words into writings. They are equally about the past that is written about and the writing that brings it to life. In other words, they deal with the creation of the past as a text.

The making of historical texts is often the work of outsiders. But mostly it originates with communities themselves. What ethnography has learned better than history is that societies do not have to wait for official interpreters to come along before they make the political choice that leads to a preference for one type of retrospective over another. Writing is one way of giving shape to the past. In the West, for better or worse, it is the accepted way.

In bringing about this understanding, writing is in many respects like reading. But there is a difference. Each of us reads with his or her own eyes. Writing also begins as a private experience, and it remains so if what is written is not read. But in principle texts are public. They are accessible to those who read as well as to those who are read to. Moreover, the writing is not just the written, the product: it is whatever goes into the making of it. And all that this activity can tell us is relevant to an accounting of the past.

Writings are made out of words, or out of what Mikhail Bakhtin calls verbal texts. A major theme of this collection is what happens when there is a shift from the oral to the written in the field of religion and society. My inquiry concerns the framing devices, the process of legitimation, and the influences on behavior (see chapter 8).

It is important to recognize that this type of transformation can take place in two ways (see chapter 1). For instance, in the literate sectors of an archaic society, an individual can supersede inherited laws, customs, and norms by claiming to obey a direct, verbal call from God. Conversely, in a community that functions orally, a scripture that is said to contain the thoughts of a deity can have a radical effect on an individual's actions.

The authenticating instruments in each case are words or writings. But they operate by what Wittgenstein calls referential magic. They derive their power to bring about change from their contexts and conventions. What unsettle patterns of conduct are the timing and the circumstances of the displacement. As a result, the unsatisfied needs of one audience transcend the satisfied needs of another (see chapter 2).

Between the late ancient world and the thirteenth century there were a number of occasions when words superseded texts and vice versa. In each instance, the social implications must be carefully evaluated. But within this period of Western history there was also a general reorientation of outlook.

The ancient world was by and large a literate society. This means, minimally, that language had a fixed grammar, schools employed books, and many institutions had written laws. When Christianity made its appearance, it did so in a world that assumed a large degree of literacy as the norm. Yet its spokesmen maintained that they were in direct dialogue with God. The gospels are filled with metaphors that extol the Word. These expressions were deliberately contrasted with one extreme of the literate mentality in the hellenistic world, Judaism. Christianity met Roman literacy on a similar level. Just as the Christian "spirit" took the place of the alleged Jewish "letter," so it rose to the challenge of what was due to Caesar by disenfranchising Roman civilization through a new form of discourse. This is another facet of the direct dialogue with God (see chapter 7).

Some centuries later, when Christianity was introduced into the largely oral Germanic culture north of the Mediterranean, a different chapter of this symbolic drama was enacted. For this oral faith had now become a scriptural religion. Not only were the gospels texts. Christianity took over the legal framework of Rome, which it transformed into canon law. In the task of converting the Germanic peoples, the authority of scripture was its chief weapon. Literacy meant legitimacy. Literacy also implied a causal agency that superseded the "magic" of the oral world, as frequent miracles confirmed. By an irony of history, Christianity fulfilled its mission in the West by means of a grammatical, and later theological, literalism that differed in function, but not in form, from the concern for the law that was its original complaint against Judaism. Obviously Jewish legalism and Christian literalism were not the same. But the gulf that separated them was small compared to the one that divides a literate community from a genuinely oral one. I should add that Christianity placed the literal before the spiritual for pragmatic reasons, which Judaism did not. In the largely oral culture of the early Middle Ages, Latin was the unique language of both grammar and scripture. To teach grammar was to teach the letter of the Word.

Clearly, then, in the passage from hellenistic Roman and Jewish antiquity to the Christian Middle Ages, the oral did not simply replace the written. Nor did the literate orality of the gospels and the primary orality of the Germanic tribesmen merge. By an inversion of symbols, one type of scripturalism succeeded another. Christianity won the West partly through the content of the Bible, which it reinterpreted to suit its needs. But it also conquered by exploiting a proven means of communication.

The consequence of this change was momentous. It provided a legal, institutional, and societal framework for the interdependence of oral and written traditions. There was no orality without an implied textuality: there was no literacy without the primal force of the spoken word. Much of the subsequent dynamism of literature and society, in the sacred as well as the secular sphere, arose from the continual reworking of this arrangement, which was mechanized, but not substantively altered, by printing. For the discovery of the later ancient world was not the difference between the visible and aural forms of language. It was an idea of the text that included both.

The transition from Judaism to Christianity was not an absolute beginning. The issues appeared as early as Plato's *Phaedrus* and *Seventh Letter*, in which the inherent fragility of writing was criticized. But most of Plato's writings disappeared at the end of antiquity; they were not known again in the West until the Renaissance. His discussion of writing was not an influence in the lengthy intervening period. Moreover, Plato's distrust of writing is at one end of a scale: scripturalism and the secular faith in literacy are at the other. The critical turning-point in the West was the adoption by Christianity of the Greek connection between being and speaking in concert with the Jewish custom of representing divine knowledge in sacred texts. The transformation is already advanced in St.

Paul. At the end of the ancient world, the basic ideas are summed up in Augustine's *De Doctrina Christiana*, whose fourth book, completed in 426–27, advocates the spreading of the Word through the preaching of its written message.

II

As this brief overview suggests, the study of oral and written traditions is not an invention of the modern age. However, since the nineteenth century, there has been a widespread growth of interest among historians in the media of communications and their influence. An early sign of this was the Romantic rediscovery of the allegedly oral, spontaneous, and "popular" culture of the Middle Ages (see chapter 4). Medieval evidence thereby came to underpin one of the prevalent myths about literacy—namely, that ages of writing are normally preceded by ages of the spoken word. By the mid-nineteenth century, as history entered the academic curriculum and the study of religion was slowly demystified, disciplined analyses of specific issues made their appearance, first in hermeneutics, philology, and anthropology, and later in linguistics, developmental psychology, and some branches of literary criticism (see chapter 3).

The result of this century or more of work on orality and literacy has been to leave two large theses in the field. One is a strong thesis; the other is composed of a variety of weak theses.

The strong thesis is usually proposed for the advent of literacy in a previously oral society, and it runs as follows. If there has been no writing before, then it is possible to speculate on the influence that the introduction of literacy has on life and thought. Changes in mentality may be the result of bringing reading and writing to a society for the first time.

The weak thesis is somewhat different: it attempts to account for the interaction of the oral and the written after the initial step is taken. It assumes that a knowledge of writing is not completely new. More writing is merely being introduced into a society that already has some texts. Therefore, cognitive change cannot be based on a straightforward transition from nonliteracy to literacy. This is not even the central issue. The focus of interest lies in the way in which speech and writing answer to different social priorities. In a community that knows reading and writing, the advent of more literacy is a force for change. But one must also look at geographical, linguistic, economic, and political factors. One must take account of gender.

There are some observations that can be made about these theses. They are both literacy hypotheses, although in different ways. They are never made about orality alone. Also, it is easy to overstate the strong thesis. This results in a schematic picture of cultural change, in which complex historical developments are reduced to binary opposites like McLuhan's "hot" and "cool" media. A further limitation arises from the attempt to use the one or the other in isolation to account for social transformations. A balanced approach requires both. To a purist in theory, this may seem untidy. But it best reflects what we know about communications media: they do not bring about mutations in society without accompanying reflections on what change means.

Is there a way of uniting the strong and weak theses? I think so, but a certain flexibility in outlook is necessary if the marriage is to work.

The strong thesis sees orality and literacy as differing mentalities. The terms are just parallels for dichotomies like prelogical/logical, irrational/rational, magical/scientific, and traditional/modern. The advantage of this perspective is that it offers a vocabulary capable of dealing with evolutionary change. For the strong thesis views orality and literacy both as states of mind and as stages of culture.

However necessary this type of thinking is, it is incomplete. It

6

only accounts for the ground-breaking ceremonies in culture. To describe what comes afterwards, we need the weak theses. These interpret the oral and the written as forms of expression and performance. Emphasis is shifted away from ultimate origins and global mentalities and toward the everyday challenges and responses of social life. In this view, culture does not resemble an evolutionary tree; it is more like a game, in which a central place is reserved for interactive play.

In most studied societies—whether they are dead societies that we learn about from their literary remains or living societies that we can observe in the field—the strong and weak theses are simultaneously applicable. There is a large-scale shift from the oral to the written, and with it the rise of a more literate sector in culture. This sort of change took place long ago in Greece, Israel, the Western Middle Ages, and in the rise of Islam, with specific consequences for each civilization. It is still taking place in corners of Asia, Africa, and South America, where tribal and peasant communities are experiencing their first contact with Western education.

Yet, while literate ways of thinking make headway, thought itself does not stand still. The coming of literacy heralds a new style of reflection. Individuals are aware of what is taking place, and this awareness influences the way they think about communication before reading and writing. An oral past that never existed may be brought to life and traditions given a legendary prehistory when they are only a couple of generations old. Alternately, a scriptural tradition that is the by-product of recent menaces to the preservation of verbal texts may be posited as eternal. In areas like this, the spoken and the written do not operate only in the external world. They also provoke subjective reactions. They provide us with insights into a system of mental representations in which "orality" and "literacy" play the roles of categories that classify a wide variety of social conventions having little or nothing to do with whether they are spoken or written.

7

If one takes ancient and medieval society as one's laboratory, the two types of transition can be seen to be acting together. There was a distinct shift from the oral to the written, for instance, when Frankish customs were replaced after the ninth century by the literate jurisprudence of Roman and canon law. But there were also subtle changes in traditions that were becoming more self-consciously literate, as when the *chanson de geste* was written down and read aloud from a text in response to the needs of a sedentary courtly audience, while retaining the oral-formulaic style of its past. It is not difficult to see how a movement from the oral to the written can alter the way in which a society sees itself. It is less often recognized that archaisms or anachronisms, taking the form of the oral or the written, can also influence perceptions, attitudes, and practices.

III

The strong and weak theses on orality and literacy reflect a broad debate in the human sciences on the status of texts. Recent philosophy, literary criticism, and historical writing mirror the issues in different ways. However, as the question of texts is raised in this volume, the clearest framing of positions arises in anthropology.

There are two sides to the debate in anthropology. On the one, we have the ethnographers, who go about the necessary work of recording. On the other, we have interpretive anthropology, which asks questions about the texts and contexts of this writing, as does Clifford Geertz, as well as about genres, genders, politics, and authorial stances. Similarly, there are two points of view in oral and literate studies. There are early strong theses, like that of Eric Havelock, and there are later weak theses in which the academics who study the problems are assumed to be part of the process that has given basic values to the concepts that define the field.

Let us not confuse the questions. The issues tackled by the

strong thesis are the changes in societies that take place independently of the observer. This is the area of inquiry, as Jack Goody puts it, between "the logic of writing" and "the organization of society." It does not matter whether changes take place from within through forms of thought or from the outside in ways visible in cultural history. Societies do not evolve at the same rate nor in the same way under the influence of given media of communications. Some welcome new technologies, others resist. The advantage of the strong thesis is its lateral perspective on these developments. It assumes that something is really happening. The object of research is to compare what is taking place in one society, or branch of it, with what is taking place elsewhere. Generalizations result from the comparison of empirical findings.

As an ethnography of the present or the past, however, this point of view needs to be qualified. There are limits to the usefulness of the terms *orality* and *literacy* arising from their history and from their ideological connections.

The present range of meaning of the pair does not exist much before the nineteenth century. The concept of orality was brought into being by folklore and studies of popular culture, while the notion of literacy was inseparable from programs in general education. The intellectual origins of both ideas are Western, and to non-Westerners they smack of ethnocentrism. They may tell us about other cultures, but they tell us a lot more about our relationship to them. Worse, it may be asked whether, as literates, we understand orality as anything but the opposite of literacy. Employing these concepts, we thus run the risk of intellectual imperialism among peoples that do not share our faith in the value of writing. Finally, orality and literacy occupy different positions in the politics of the academy. Orality is mainly identified with the study of poetry. Also, studies of orality are sometimes nostalgic pleas on behalf of traditions that have disappeared or are threatened. Such works imply a rejection of the literate norms of today in favor of an earlier, "purer" state of mind. Consequently they have a utopian, even countercultural, air. By contrast, studies of literacy have strong links with notions of economic and social progress, whence the place of education in the classical political economy of Adam Smith, Marx, and Mill, as well as in the ideologies of development, which seek to make other cultures literate in our terms.

Criticisms of the concepts of "orality" and "literacy" have much merit, but it is easy to carry them too far. Linguistics teaches that discourse has many ways of fixing the relations between sound and sense without the aid of script. Societies that lack writing nonetheless record, remember, and transmit verbal texts whose grip on norms, values, and traditions is no less tenacious than that of writing. Non-Western scriptural societies exist in China, India, and elsewhere in Asia. The presence of an indigenous system of writing is no guarantee against the political use of the written word, any more than the absence of "capitalism" is a guarantee against exploitation. True, in the West, oral literatures have not had the prestige they deserve. Even the orality of Homer, as demonstrated in the pioneering studies of Milman Parry (see chapter 8), is soon forgotten by the student of higher criticism. Oral literature in formerly colonial lands has had to adopt the outsider's literary formats in order to be heard. So have women. Ideally, one would like to overcome these problems by replacing the terms *orality* and *literacy* with something more neutral—within these essays, I suggest that we speak of the uses of oral or written texts—but changing the vocabulary does not alter the basic issue, which concerns publicly acknowledged referential tools.

A less radical, more useful type of criticism is to propose that to be literate in any sense is also to be literary. There is no way of separating events from the language in which they are described. It is not reality we question, but our manner of representing it. Societies may tell different stories, but when we come to retell them, we use a limited range of explanatory and persuasive techniques. History used to be a branch of rhetoric (see chapter 1). If we wish to understand what is said in old or new social narratives, literary analysis is still essential. For there are no tales without implied narrators and audiences: the social function of texts, as well as the literary function of societies, consists of maintaining the metaphysical links. What is more, stories do not convince us by their arguments but by their lifelikeness (see chapter 2). They may be verifiable, if we can get at the "facts"; but mainly they are believable. Why narratives conform to our readerly and psychological expectations is not fully understood. But pieces of the picture are now clear, and among the potent influences are subtle relations between voice and text in establishing verisimilitude. These connections need to be further explored.

The approach I advocate has its limitations too. One of them is the removing of needed energies from fields of research, such as medieval history, in which there remains much recording and describing to be done. But it has an overriding value as well. This is to question some of our assumptions about the meaning of the notion of literature, whether oral or written. The idea is clearly invented. What we want to know is where its origins lie, and, if possible, why the concept took hold when it did. One thesis places its beginnings in the eighteenth century, when the leisured classes of industrializing societies took up reading on a large scale for the first time. But, in my view, this historical perspective is too short. Behind the assumptions of the newly formed public for popular classics lay a long tradition. The pathways all lead backwards in time to a moment when *litteratura*, the Latin predecessor of the modern notion, ceased to mean phonetics and grammar and started to mean what we know as literature. This signifies the opening of a new chapter in relations between texts, verbal or written, and nascent European societies.

I add a final note on two other disciplines employed in this volume, hermeneutics and the sociology of Max Weber. Ancient hermeneutics is one of the points of departure for the study of orality and literacy. As the concept passed from antiquity to the Middle Ages, *hermenēuein* gradually came to mean the interpretation of what is said in texts. Contemporary hermeneutics, as it evolved in Dilthey, Heidegger, Gadamer, and Ricoeur, has proven to be a useful tool in analysing this relationship. Yet, from a historian's perspective, it is a limited one. Hermeneutics is biased in favor of the spoken word, to which writings are normally reduced, despite the lesson of history that oral and literate traditions have differing social and institutional properties. Another weakness derives from phenomenology. This is the notion of preconceptual thinking, about which no genuine history can be written. But there is a greater limitation still. In general, hermeneutics pays more attention to the definition of the reader than to the variety of reading experiences illustrated by history or ethnography. We need a general theory of interpretation as a set of guidelines. But if we are to understand how reading actually evolved from the ancient world to the present, we also have to accommodate the research of historians like Paul Saenger, Elizabeth Eisenstein, Natalie Davis, and Roger Chartier. Hermeneutics is a valuable aid in working out the intertextual relations that historians often overlook. It is less helpful in locating the root causes of change: it does not tell us why oral or written traditions are superseded, or how the timing of the shift can bring about a rethinking of mentality.

The contemporary position in hermeneutics that is most accessible to historians is that of Paul Ricoeur (see chapter 5). The strength of his approach lies in placing the text, rather than speaking or writing alone, at the center of the problem. By contrast, Foucault's notion of *discours* channels a similar concern into a discussion of the vehicles of social control by which ideas, acting within like assimilated texts, influence group behavior over time. I prefer to call this mutual understanding a textual community. But there is also a difference between Foucault's notion and my own. His, as I see it, is the close neighbor of a hard concept, and, as a consequence, from a historical point of view, it has a certain inflexibility. Mine is intended to be an empirical generalization: if it never quite rises to the level of a collective idea, it nonetheless reflects cases of behavioral deviation in their considerable variety. In textual communities, concepts appear first as they are acted out by individuals or groups in everyday life. Only later, and within norms structured by texts, is there a collective consciousness. I do not claim superiority for this approach over hermeneutics or the study of *discours*. But it does make the practical business of writing history easier.

My reasons for taking up Max Weber are different. They arise from the view that the future of oral and literate studies lies in an accommodation with the acquired understanding of earlier social theory (see chapter 6).

Among classical theorists, Weber remains the most influential. Yet there are two hiatuses in his otherwise encyclopedic grasp of the social sciences in his time. One is an ignorance of the factual history of the Middle Ages, which made him unaware of the forerunners of many developments he associated with the Reformation. More significantly, Weber gave almost no place to the analysis of orality and literacy as factors capable of influencing rationalization processes over time. These lacunae amount to structural weaknesses in his outlook: the theory is deficient because of a lack of historical data, and the data that he has are therefore insufficiently conceptualized.

There are a number of areas of Weber's thinking that are clarified by a consideration of orality, literacy, and society. One is the concept of subjectively meaningful action, which can be better understood by observing the role of media of communications.

Another is the notion of "Western individualism" and its links with reading and writing. But the major potential arises from a revamping of Weber's ideas on rationalization. Just as literacy promotes universalism through a text that is disembodied and objectified by script, so it favors a certain style of rationalization in societies, one that leads to accounting systems, bureaucracy, and the other machinery of the capitalist ascendancy commanding Weber's attention. It was during the Middle Ages that the relationship between *ratio* and *scriptum* first became a liberating instrument and also a new source of subjection. We have to ask how this happened, and why.

The connection between my reflections on Weber and the other essays in this volume is the idea of the text. The term is used so widely, and so indiscriminately, that something should be said about the way it is employed in what follows.

As I see it, it is not possible to say precisely what is or is not a text. No definition is sufficiently comprehensive to cover all cases. The concept of the text is merely a more practical intellectual tool than that of literature. It is not neutral, for no idea is. Nor is it more capable than "literature" of reflecting the genetic possibilities of both oral and written development. It is more useful because it is more manageable. Societies may be chartered by myths that we call literature, but no society is ever motivated by more than a small part of its heritage at a given time or place. Action is normally based on small units—scripts, scenarios, and parts of bigger narratives. The historian or ethnographer must read a whole society's archive, but he or she must also listen carefully for those key texts.

Yet even allowing for its advantage over notions like literature, we must also recognize that the idea of the text is a homespun, Western one. It was the product of specific historical circumstances. We do not find any talk of it before the scriptural religions. Most of the critical developments took place in the later ancient world and the Middle Ages. Thinking on the subject is already perceptible in Philo, and it had solidified by the time of Augustine and Boethius. They, in turn, look forward to the proliferation of views on textuality in the Middle Ages and beyond. Building on ancient foundations, but isolated from the Greek philosophy that gave those foundations their strength, the medievals were forced to find their own solutions to the problem of reading, writing, and society. The purpose of these essays is to provide some glimpses of this fascinating evolution, and to draw attention to the role of the Middle Ages in the formation of postmedieval theories under discussion in our time. For if there are thoughts from the past that still have a hold on us, these are certainly among them.

CHAPTER ONE

HISTORY, LITERATURE, TEXTUALITY

It is possible nowadays, as it has not been in the immediate past, to envisage serious cooperation between the study of history and literature. This happy state of affairs has been brought about by a number of complementary forces. Among intellectual historians, positivistic assumptions, where they are not under attack, appear to be dying a natural death. Accounting for what actually took place is recognized to be only a part of the story. The other part is the record of what individuals thought was taking place, and the ways in which their feelings, perceptions, and narratives influenced or were influenced by the events they experienced. Among critics of literature one finds a growing interest in history. This is no longer a mere summary of factual and biographical information, as it often was in the period before new criticism. Under the guidance of linguistics, semiotics, and hermeneutics, the new historicism recognizes the interdependence of all modes of interpretation, as well as their inevitable transience.

Some of the factors contributing to the renewed awareness of the historical dimension have arisen from within historical research, like the study of *mentalité* in *Annales* or the more diluted tradition of thinking about ideas and society that has filtered down through Dilthey, Max Weber, and the Frankfurt School. Other causes lie outside the field of history. In general, twentieth-century historiography has had to adapt itself from a cultural climate of self-confidence to one of self-questioning. No less than political idealism, the pure history of ideas belonged to a period of social and political consensus. As the intellectual universe has become pluralistic, historical relativism has become more fashionable. Yet a considerable gap exists between what many intellectual historians would like to be doing and what they have been trained to do. To borrow Heidegger's terms, most are instructed how to deal with "documents" rather than "works"–that is, with repositories of information rather than structured texts. Competent to handle the factual side of research, and, until recently, secure in their assumptions about historical objectivity, they have paid little attention to aspects of cultural analysis such as *langue* and *parole*, synchrony and diachrony, or narrative and discourse. Despite a revival of interest in oral and written forms of expression among historians, it is difficult to see a clear role for the study of language within historical methodology.[1]

Other factors contributing to the potential cooperation of history and literature have arisen from recent trends in literary criticism. An important principle in structuralism, emphasized by Barthes, is the separation of the author and authorial intentions from the text that results from the act of writing. The text may thus be seen to have a set of depersonalized relations with other texts, and all texts, including historical ones, are placed on an equal footing. In semiotics, a similar goal is achieved by a different route, since there is no valid way of distinguishing between the historical and literary uses of signs. Hans Robert Jauss's notion of "horizons of expectation" implies a serious program of literary history, as, in a parallel manner, does the study of intertextuality, which, like *Rezeptionsästhetik*, denies the autonomy of the text and suggests that, through the reading process, signification results from the imposition of prior knowledge upon present meaning. For Marxist criticism the issues of subject and object and of historical determination remain primary. But even here the problem is no longer seen as a simplistic demonstration of relations between production and consumption. One can even see in Derrida's rejection of Foucault's strong emphasis on discontinuity a return to a type of sequentialist thinking. If deconstruction is to work, one must assume that the spoken and written acts by which meaning is created operate over time.

The period of history that has contributed the most to reviving a formal inquiry into relations between the literary and historical dimensions of culture is the Middle Ages. Medievalists have made among the most lasting contributions to the study of *mentalité*: one thinks of its inventors, Marc Bloch and Lucien Febvre, as well as Paul Alphandéry and, more recently, Jacques Le Goff, Emmanuel Le Roy Ladurie, Jean Delumeau, and Georges Duby. On the literary side, it is worth recalling that figures as influential as E. R. Curtius, Erich Auerbach, and Mikhail Bakhtin all spent a part of their careers in medieval research. So has Paul Zumthor.

These are direct debts. There are also indirect relationships, often undiscussed, between recent trends in intellectual history and revivals of interest in medieval culture. The contemporary rethinking of anthropology, literary criticism, and the history of ideas is part of a more general rebirth in the field of language and culture. In France, this involves structuralism and poststructuralism; in England, the philosophical implications of Wittgenstein and J. L. Austin; and in Germany the questioning of the status of hermeneutics raised in the exchange of views between Hans-Georg Gadamer and Jürgen Habermas.

The common ground of these diverse approaches is textuality. If one attempts to give a historical context to the linguistic concerns they raise, the natural starting-point is the period in which Europe became a society that used texts on a large scale. This was the Middle Ages. To put the matter another way: if competence and performance in language are important for understanding how culture works in contemporary society, we cannot pretend to have a reasonable grasp of the issues without returning to the moment in time when texts became a recognizable force in an evolutionary process that has continued uninterrupted down to our own day. For the student of the Middle Ages there is a certain irony in this. Paradoxically, if one wishes to understand medieval culture on its own terms, to the degree that this is possible, one is obliged to adopt methods that are medieval in origin, but have only recently been rediscovered by investigations in linguistics, philosophy, anthropology, and psychoanalysis, disciplines unconcerned with the medieval epoch and as a rule unhistorical in their methods.

Understanding how a textually oriented society came into being presupposes a basic chronology of medieval literacy. If we take as our point of departure the admittedly arbitrary date of A.D. 1000, we see both oral and written traditions operating simultaneously in European culture, sometimes working together, but more often in separate zones, such as oral custom and written law. This was an eclectic heritage: it arose from Greek and Roman education, from Jewish scripturalism as transformed by early Christians, and from Germanic languages and institutions, which originally lacked writing. However, beginning as early as the ninth century, and gaining considerable momentum after the turn of the eleventh, a widespread transformation began to take place. Latin literacy was permanently established on the Continent, while in Ireland and England, the vernacular literate culture was strengthened.

As the written word came to play a more important role in law, administration, and commerce, existing oral traditions either declined or adapted to a new environment. In some cases this amounted to a simple evolution from one type of expression to another; in others, it was a readjustment to something loosely resembling the state of affairs that existed in the ancient world. But in neither case did oral culture disappear. Its apparent diminishing in vitality was in fact a realignment, enabling it to function in a reference system based on texts. As a result, we observe a new hermeneutics of society and culture emerging slowly in western Europe. Its salient feature is that it is simultaneously oral *and* written. Performative acts in language remained verbal, and individualistic, as they had always been. But they were increasingly contextualized by writing in a manner that implied shared values, assumptions, and modes of explanation.

The texts were not always written down, but they were invariably understood as if they were. An invisible scripture seemed to lurk behind everything one said. Meaning gravitated to this written type of reference, rather than to the sense of the spoken alone; and what had been expressed in gestures, rituals, and physical symbols became imbedded in a set of interpretive structures involving grammars, notations, and lexica. The spoken and the written were drawn into closer interdependence than they had been at any time since the end of the ancient world. The changes were of the type Braudel calls *la longue durée*. They announced the birth of the European vernacular languages, as well as problems in the area of language and culture that were to recur in different forms in the following centuries. Among these were the dichotomy of popular versus learned tradition; the rise of allegory, with its interest in inner meaning; and, via thinkers like Abelard, the issue of the nominal and the real in language, together with a consideration of the conventional aspects of linguistic interchange that Wittgenstein calls "forms of life." The rise of textuality also led to the articulation of relations between the producers and consumers of culture, as the focus of their interest was now the same externalized object. All this amounted to a transformation of the system of exchange and communication. Via written transcriptions, the real or abstract reading public became the frame of reference for the interpretation of works of literature, philosophy, and theology, and, through intertextuality, for the interpretation of experience.

Any consideration of the uses of literacy immediately raises the issue of power relations in society. If a new means of communication makes its appearance, who are its patrons? If new knowledge is produced, who controls it and for what ends?

The answer to these questions is not as simple as would first appear. Let us first consider the problem theoretically, then look at a practical example.

What is notable about early efforts to theorize about the issues is a preference for a macrosociological approach. An attempt was usually made to match the content of ideological systems with the economic and social background of the participants. The weaknesses of this method have been often enough demonstrated by the intellectual left and right to need no further emphasis. The successors to the early *Soziologie des Wissens*, such as Lucien Goldmann's genetic structuralism, inevitably abandoned the lofty ideal of describing sociological totalities and focused instead on the more manageable dimension of social groups whose actual productions and literary relations could be empirically studied. The advent of structuralism both abetted and detracted from this development. On the positive side, structuralism desubjectivized literary experience, as I have noted. But, by demoting authorship, structuralism also weakened the tentatively established connections between literature and society and took the entire debate one step away from the living world of utterance, discourse, and action. The popularity of structuralism was partly attributable to a frustration that was felt over the failure of the Marxist sociology of knowledge (Max Weber having made little impact on French thinkers in the fifties). The leading proponents seemed to say: if social relations cannot be revealed through texts, then we will study the properties of texts for their own sake and pretend that we are studying society. Poststructuralism continued this trend. In Derrida, criticism, by its very definition, does not move beyond the text. The door to social analysis is virtually closed, and discussion is limited to what are essentially alternative interpretations. The rise and fall of the sociology of knowledge posed two problems for medievalists. The older approaches, beginning in Marx, and developing in different ways in Mannheim and Lukács, depended on an oversimplified view of the Middle Ages in which the peasants, the bourgeoisie, and the aristocracy were portrayed as having watertight mentalities issuing in specific literary, theological, or artistic genres. But there was an even more basic problem. In pushing *Weltanschauung* back into the Middle Ages, students often made the assumption that the term *society* in a medieval context corresponds to what we know as "industrial," or "American," society. This was stretching an ideal-type a little too far. There were ethnic, linguistic, and protonational ties in the Middle Ages. But this was not a society in the post-Kantian sense of the term. For the implicit and explicit boundaries that divided and united men and women were distinctly unmodern in character. And it follows that, if we cannot speak of a society in the larger sense, a macrosociology of knowledge is of little value. By the use of such global concepts, an inadequate characterization of medieval civilization was introduced into the contemporary consciousness, where it still appears in textbooks and encyclopedias. Worse, medievalists attempted for some decades to apply a methodology inherently inappropriate for inquiring into the society they had set themselves to study. A younger generation turned away from such constructions and opted for the study of ideas and society using more carefully defined agendas such as folklore, anthropology, and hermeneutics.

One potential approach is to investigate the relationships between individuals in groups that are actually using texts for literary or social purposes, while at the same time paying close attention to the historical context of their actions as well as to consequences. The point of departure for this method is Weber's notion of subjectively meaningful social action, to which one adds a distinction between intersubjectivity, a feature of minds, and intertextuality, an aspect of writings. What results is the analysis of what I call "textual communities," which are microsocieties organized around the common understanding of a script.

The problem can be put as follows. The rise of a more literate society in the eleventh century automatically increased the number of authors, readers, and copiers of texts everywhere in Europe, and, as a consequence, the number of persons engaged in the study of texts for the purpose of changing the behavior of the individual or group. This, *in nuce*, was the rationale behind much reformist and some orthodox religious agitation, to say nothing of communal associations and guilds. These textual communities were not entirely composed of literates. The minimal requirement was just one literate, the *interpres*, who understood a set of texts and was able to pass his message on verbally to others. By a process of absorption and reflection the behavioral norms of the group's other members were eventually altered. The manner in which the individuals behaved toward each other and the manner in which the group looked upon those it considered to be outsiders were derived from the attitudes formed during the period of initiation and education. The unlettered and semilettered members thereby conceptualized a link between textuality, as the script for the enactment of behavioral norms, and rationality, as the alleged reasonableness of those norms. Note that this link itself may not have been articulated in a literate fashion; thus, while the basis of action was textual, it was not always recognized as such. To further complicate matters, ritual observances were frequently preserved. Within the literate mentality, they were thought to be archaic. Individuals belonging to textual communities existed in a halfway house between literacy and nonliteracy. Their reaction to forces for change is typical, not only of the European experience, but also of contemporary societies encountering Western education for the first time.

I will return to the question of theory later in this volume.[2] It is now time to take up an example. My choice is the Waldensians, a small Christian sect that survives today in Piedmont as the Chiesa Evangelica Valdese. Older Protestant historians saw them as an uncorrupted form of Christianity, founded by St. Paul, which had miraculously avoided the early medieval Church's involvement in temporal affairs. During the Middle Ages they were sometimes associated with the heresy of Claudius of Turin, and inquisitors often confused them with the Albigensians.

But the most important feature of the "origin" of the Waldensians is not described by either medieval or early modern commentators. This is the role of literacy. Its function can be observed if we examine the two complementary accounts of the sect's beginnings. The earlier and less reliable of them is the anonymous chronicle of Laon for the years 1173 and 1178.[3] The later account is a chapter in the unfinished *De Septem Donis Spiritus Sanctus* of the Dominican inquisitor, Etienne de Bourbon, who died in Lyons in 1262.[4] Etienne's version has the advantage of reflecting personal interviews with two priests who acted respectively as copyist and translator for the sect's acknowledged founder, a rich moneylender named Peter Waldo.

The story of Waldensian origins in the Laon chronicle is considered by most historians to consist of a little fact and a lot of fiction.[5] Briefly, it recounts how Peter Waldo, inspired by a public recital of the life of St. Alexis, gave away his money and property, left his wife and two daughters, began to perform acts of public charity, and eventually adopted a life of rigorous poverty and itinerant preaching. Like Alexis he was converted at home: there, the chronicler states, he had invited the wandering singer whom he had heard reciting the life in order to learn more about the legendary youth who achieved salvation after undergoing exile, penance, and self-abnegation. On the morning after the meeting at his house, Waldo went to the local seminary. He sought "counsel for his soul" and asked the local master of biblical studies "the surest and most perfect way of approaching God." He was reminded of Jesus's words, "If you would be perfect, go and sell all that you have" (Matt. 19:21).[6]

Etienne de Bourbon does not repeat this narrative, but he is more emphatic on the role played by literacy in Waldo's spiritual awakening. Waldo, he relates, although not well versed in letters himself, nonetheless desired a deeper understanding of the gospels. He made contact with two priests: one, Stephen of Anse, translated passages of the Bible for him into French, while the other, Bernard Ydros, acted as his scribe and recorded them. Waldo thereby acquired vernacular transcripts of many of the books of the Bible, together with a number of authoritative commentaries. These, Etienne adds, he studied in detail, making them the basis for his ascetic way of life and his search for inner perfection.[7]

If read side by side, the two accounts tell us much about the role of literacy in the sect's founding and how it was first interpreted. There are three stages in the making of a community:

1. Oral contact. In the Laon chronicle, this takes place through a jongleur; in Etienne de Bourbon, Waldo hears the gospel. However, it should be noted that both of these oral experiences are attached to a textual backdrop. The jongleur sings an oral text; the preachers read a text of the gospels.

2. An educative process. In the Laon version, Waldo seeks counsel for his soul; in Etienne, he orders a translation of the Bible into the vernacular (*in romano, in vulgari*). This leads to the study of vernacular texts, their commitment to memory, and preaching by Waldo or his delegates, sometimes in public.

3. Finally, the historicizing of the community—that is, giving it

a past. This is accomplished in the Laon chronicle through intertextuality. For there are two texts of renunciation. One is the *Life of St. Alexis*, which Waldo hears. The other is the *Life of St. Anthony*, to which a reference is obliquely made by the local master in theology. The passage of Matthew that he quotes to Waldo is the same text as Anthony heard as he passed before his village church just a short time after inheriting his familial estate.[8] Medieval readers would have recognized this allusion, and Waldo would thereby be associated with an archetypical saint's life.

The most interesting point of agreement between the two versions of Waldo's story arises from the fact that neither he nor his followers appear to have been literate in the normal medieval sense of understanding Latin. The Laon chronicle mentions only oral-aural contact with both vernacular and Latin literacy. Waldo, it states, wanted to hear the jongleur (*audire curavit*); he was fascinated by the example as it was told to him; and he begged advice from the local master, seeking, it would appear, not reading matter, but a surer and more perfect way to salvation. Etienne de Bourbon presents a more nuanced view, colored perhaps by his interest in exegesis and preaching. In his version the key statement is this: Waldo, "although not particularly literate, on hearing the gospel, was desirous to know what the biblical text said. He entered into an agreement with two priests: one of them rendered the passages in the spoken language, while the other wrote down what was dictated." What is notable is that the desire for a vernacular text on which to base interpretation was inspired by ignorance, not understanding. There was no continuity with a previous literate tradition; rather, there was discontinuity. Linguistic disjunction brought about the production of a new text, one that, Etienne notes, Waldo read, reread, and internalized.

The church had no objection to the Waldensians dispossessing themselves of their wealth and devoting their efforts to aiding the poor. But they also formed a type of community that Etienne could not accept. The offending ingredient was public preaching, which, unlicensed, threatened the local episcopal monopoly on the communication of the Word. Of what did the violation consist? Just this: based on an agreed meaning for passages of the gospels among the members of the group—which we may call the real text, as opposed to the biblical original or the many verbal interpretations that were possible—the Waldensians took to propagating their own message. Their authority arose from their common understanding, not from the inherited traditions of the past. They differed from orthodoxy not in their doctrines but in their way of arriving at them. And they spread their ideas effectively. Etienne shows his distaste for their preaching in the streets and squares of Lyons. Waldo apparently attracted men and women to the gospel through his personal ability to recreate its narrative with vividness and conviction. He dared, the Dominican commentator adds, to send persons of the lowest social station to preach in nearby villages: men and women alike, illiterate and uneducated (*idiotae et illiteratae*), they wandered about, entered homes, and preached in churches as well as in public, everywhere arousing popular sentiment and encouraging others to follow their lead.[9]

"There was a Franciscan touch," Malcolm Lambert notes, "in his religious passion, throwing money in the street [and] rejecting the usurious business methods that had brought him wealth."[10] The observation seems natural enough in historical perspective. But the accounts of the sect's origins also raise other issues. Waldo's actions were not isolated, nor was the narrative of the Laon chronicle. Both can be thought of as part of the network of expectations in the Lyons preacher's immediate audience and in the minds of his later followers, including those who took only an intellectual interest in the events.

This is not a question of sources (that is, of literary or historical exemplars), although these may well exist. Rather it concerns the relationship of Waldo's conversion both as an experience and as a text to a body of attitudes and assumptions in his contemporaries' minds. It is both personal and impersonal: it involves Waldo's charismatic authority, his individual living out of a New Testament theme, as well as his audience's reaction to an already contextualized set of thoughts and actions. These had begun to manifest themselves over half a century before through wandering preachers such as Bernard of Tiron, Robert of Arbrissel, and Norbert of Xanten; they took a different direction in frustrated Gregorians of the next generation such as Henry of Lausanne and Arnold of Brescia; and they were finally enacted against the backdrop of reformed monasticism and the rise of Catharism. In other words, there is a whole series of previously enacted situations, some recorded, others unrecorded, all forming part of the collective memory and allowing Waldo's actions to be perceived as a meaningful pattern even by those who, like Etienne de Bourbon, opposed his ultimate goals.

The pattern is in part explicit, as dramatized by his leaving his wealth and family, and in part implicit, since it involves an inner code of conduct through which outer behavior can be interpreted and measured. In a medieval setting, one can propose, the expectations usually associated with intertextuality were not only, and perhaps not chiefly, found in subsequent readers, even though, as a historical picture of heresy was gradually built up through such accounts, they were able to reenter the semantic space in which the original events were thought to have taken place. Rather the echo is most easily found in Waldo's contemporaries and immediate followers, who, if employing oral methods, participated in what was largely a literate experience. In that primal moment of interaction the discourse acquired its operative historical dimension. For men and women not only presumed to understand the convert's actions but, without consciously thinking about what they were doing, modeled their behavior on his.

By the example of Waldensian "origins" I have tried to illustrate a basic feature of textual communities, whether these consist of religious sects, as they frequently did in the Middle Ages, or whether, in the modern context, we see them emerge as secular political associations, economically inspired social movements, or gender-related responses between readers and audiences. What is essential to realize is that there are both a historical and a literary dimension to their activity. Both are cognitive, interpretable, and narratively shaped. The historical is not isolated from the literary as fact and representation. The two aspects of the experience work together: the objectivity of the events spills over into the subjectivity of the records, perceptions, feelings, and observations. The transcribed experience also feeds back into the lived lives. In Waldo's case, it is impossible to separate his actions from a chain of reflections on earlier, similar patterns of conduct. In the type of analysis I propose, one cannot neglect the world outside the text, or reduce it, as some would prefer, to an easily manageable set of codes. The conscious reliving of an earlier text constitutes a new version of the experience, and the text, which, like the events of Waldo's life, appears as meaningful activity, narratively organized, before it is transcribed and passed on in written form. One cannot assume that the only way that a text will reveal its meaning is through exegesis, for codified signs can also appear as types of texts that are expressed in patterned behavior. Although the mediators between thought and action remain difficult to explain, no one doubts their existence. They cannot be wished away or dealt with by a sort of textual gnosticism. Nor, finally, is the question of power only one of exterior relations, such as operated between the medieval church and sectarian communities. Discourse is not so impersonal; it does not supersede normal social relations. Individuality, intentionality, and human will also have a place in the spectrum of assigned causes. The medieval religious figure like Waldo gives a latent discourse a tangible form, breathes life into it, and creates, if only briefly, a new universe of discursive space in which relations between interpreter and audience recreate the old pattern of authority and tradition anew.

CHAPTER TWO

MEDIEVAL LITERACY, LINGUISTIC THEORY, AND SOCIAL ORGANIZATION

From what has been said so far, it is clear that the study of the Middle Ages can tell us much about the development of Western ideas on language, culture, and society. This chapter elaborates that theme and tries to place it in a somewhat broader context. The essay deals with three related issues. At one end of the scale, I look at how two thinkers see the relationship between speech conventions and reality. At another, I take up the problem of changes in oral and written traditions in society that form a backdrop to these conceptualizations. Finally, I ask some questions about the contemporary view of these matters: what assumptions do we make about the Middle Ages, and how has the residue of medieval thinking influenced the modern environment of discussion?

I

We may begin by contrasting two well-known medieval notions of the sign, both of which, as it turns out, consist of successive commentaries on the opening paragraph of Aristotle's *Peri ermeneias*.

Boethius, attempting to convey the sense of the Greek text to an increasingly Latin culture, oversimplified the original. Roughly equating linguistic and material communication, he likened the imposition of meaning onto words to the impressing of the emperor's profile onto an imperial coin. A piece of money, he argued, is not only a metal object; it is also a medium of exchange that represents the value of another thing. Likewise, verbs and nouns are not only physical sounds but also linguistic conventions established for the purpose of signifying what is understood in the mind.[1]

Some six centuries after Boethius's untimely death in 525/26, Peter Abelard wrote his own set of commentaries on Aristotle and, while adhering to many of Boethius's fundamental tenets, used the *Peri eremeneias*, together with Porphyry, Priscian, and others, as the basis for a theory of language and meaning that preoccupied medieval thinkers down to William of Okham. Abelard proposed something similar to Saussure's distinction between *langue* and *parole*[2]—that is, in Aristotelian terms, a distinction between the logic of meaning, by which individual linguistic usage is understood among speakers, and the individual capacity for speaking, along with its phonetic and acoustic properties. Abelard's unique contribution to this theory was to explore the abstract and concrete character of signification and to reshape traditional thinking on universals to incorporate his ideas. In this, he anticipated not only Saussure but also the later Wittgenstein.

In contemporary linguistic terms, Boethius may be called a formalist, while Abelard's approach (which, it should be noted, changed over time) lies somewhere on the spectrum between formalism and functionalism.[3]

Despite its Aristotelian original, Boethius's linguistic theory is highly Platonist. For him, the realm of outer experience is a set of appearances concealing an inner reality of forms. Like all formalists, Boethius, as he develops his commentary on Aristotle, concentrates on the cognitive issues in language study—that is, on the relationship between words, texts, things, and thoughts. Language, therefore, is distinguishable from speech: the spoken word, whether actually spoken or written down, is the representation of an interior idea. Boethius would agree with the assessment of formalism in which speaking is seen to represent "unconscious knowledge or an abstract system of conventional signs and rules with which to construct sentences and construe meanings."[4] By implication, Boethius also argues that there is a difference between competence and performance: the ability to learn language in general lies behind the particular acquisition of a specific language. Further, while language expresses thought, spoken forms paradoxically constrain and limit thought's expression. To return to Boethius's metaphor, words are imperfect copies of ideas. Language, or rather its inner, formal reality, is an ideal, not a material original: it is not ultimately speaking but the knowing of the norms, rules, and conventions that makes communication possible.

Abelard agreed with many of these formalist presuppositions about language. But, through the application of logic to linguistic questions, he eventually arrived at a functionalist position that challenged the older formalism.[5] His view of language was in part conceptual and in part pragmatic and instrumental. Language, in his opinion, not only makes statements about the world; it also reveals essential relations in the world. In other words, language is not only an interior system partially revealed through speech; it is also what people actually do with words when talking about things and thoughts.[6] As a consequence, in Abelard, as contrasted with his predecessors, the individual speaker's intentions play a large role in how sense is made; and meaning, rather than constituting a purely objective dimension, arises in part from subjective interpretation. In fact, in Abelard, meaning is a sort of compromise between the speaker's intentions and the hearer's interpretation. Hence the distinction between reference and sense is not absolute; that is, for him, the world is not known in one way through physical objects and in another through mental objects such as ideas, images, sensations, and feelings. Indeed, Abelard directly anticipates the contemporary position that allows that words represent concepts while also maintaining that they represent pure abstractions, either as words, as propositions, or as the necessary inferences drawn from propositions. Abelard, as a consequence, does not solve the classical problem of representation through language; he attempts to bypass it by considering language as at once a replica of something else and an aspect of behavior.

In sum, for Boethius, as a formalist, language is object. For Abelard, as both formalist and functionalist, it is both object and subject. For Boethius, as a result, language is thought about in metaphors of pages, texts, and books—that is, in a context of grammatically established forms of written expression. For Abelard, by contrast, while textual matter forms part of the discussion, the realm of language is more properly linguistic and consists of language in use. His basic metaphor is the verbal text.

II

Abelard's approach to language is symptomatic of a more widespread change in attitudes in medieval culture. These, in turn, are bound up with the rebirth of literacy.

Between Boethius and Abelard, two acknowledged peaks in medieval theoretical development, the question of theory itself cannot be posed in quite such straightforward terms. It would be more appropriate to speak of an anthropological framework for understanding the problem of language, truth, and reality. For, even allowing for the revival of interest in Latin grammar during the ninth century, it would be fair to say that, between the sixth and the eleventh centuries, cultural institutions were generally thought of from an oral rather than a written standpoint; or, at best, the question of communication was looked upon from oral and written points of view at once. From the perspective of a more literate age, it is difficult to tell which side was more actively engaged in the process of acculturation. What today are considered normal literary interests—phonology, morphology, and the philosophy of language—were discussed by a tiny, largely clerical, elite, who, like the tenth-century Abbo of Fleury, found time within the monastic routine to ask searching questions about logic and meaning. But the majority of men and women in lay society, together with many of the lower clergy, carried on their daily lives with only minimal reference to the world of texts. In the eleventh century on the Continent, and in England from perhaps as early as the reign of Alfred the Great, the picture begins slowly to change. It was still possible for many to remain ignorant of letters, and in fact most did. However, it was less and less likely that they would remain out of touch with the social forces that the written word increasingly embodied. By the first quarter of the twelfth century the revival of literacy is an established fact. Men like Otto of Freising or Bernard of Chartres can philosophize about a genuine renaissance of classical antiquity, in which medieval achievement, now carried forward by its own momentum, beholds more felicitous prospects for the advancement of learning than did the ancient world.

There was no time during the early Middle Ages when interchange was entirely oral, and the lacunae in the written record must not be mistaken for more profound changes in the system of communication. But the existence, or should one say persistence, of oral traditions throughout the later, more literate period, down to and including the age of print, should also alert the student to the complexities underlying such facile oppositions as "low" and "high" culture, or "popular" and "learned." For reflections on literacy and nonliteracy are made, by and large, from the outset, exclusively by literati. The terms of reference for the discussion are overtly biased in favor of written exchange, which is in turn identified with the progress of a beneficent rationality, the latter often enveloped in Platonic obscurities.

It has been suggested more than once that such prejudices were merely the cultural equivalent of the power relations inherent in feudal society, in which the major means of production, the land, was controlled by a lay and clerical elite. But if that were the case, one must reverse a platitude of contemporary political philosophy, since the ruling ideas of the period appear to have stubbornly resisted the ideas of the ruling classes. Changes in medieval modes of discourse, like those of the present day, often took place independently of, or in opposition to, real or perceived social forces; that is to say, texts that people enacted were interdependent with, but not functionally supportive of, the social material out of which they were constructed.[7] Therefore, even allowing for the bias of literacy, the empirical exploration of relations between discourse and reality remains a primary concern. The central problem in the Middle Ages is the relation of orality to a world making ever-increasing use of texts, not only, as is obvious, in its real social interchange, but, more important, in the ontological sphere—that is, as a set of purely abstract or intellectualized models out of which any experience may potentially be interpreted.

On a philosophical level one can ask whether the distinction between "oral" and "written" dimensions of culture is valid at all, as bears witness Derrida's criticism of "the writing lesson" in Lévi-Strauss's *Tristes tropiques*.[8] From a linguistic point of view there is no very strong reason for maintaining a hard-and-fast line: a spoken discourse may contain all the structural features of a written text, and written versions, like the variant performances of a *chanson de geste*, continually absorb oral improvisations. But if, as Max Weber suggests, the sociologist or anthropologist is to deal with meaningful behavior as experienced and interpreted by the acting subject, the spokesmen for oral or written tradition from within medieval culture cannot simply be ignored for the sake of philosophic rigor. In other words, whether or not there is a real difference between the oral and the written, a good deal of the medieval and early modern perception of cultural differences is based upon the assumption that there is; and that perception, in the final analysis, is what the literary or social historian seeks to record, to discuss, and to comment upon.

In this sense, the study of oral and written traditions is at bottom an inquiry into important aspects of the socially inspired categorization of experience itself. Early medieval society was confronted with polar opposites: on the one hand, an immense range of relatively uncharted events, sensations, and emotions, and on the other, a limited number of inherited models for interpreting them, models that by and large acted as witnesses to the incomplete assimilation of the written by a foreign mentality, rather like the echoing of the Justinian codices in Salic law. Between the sixth and the eleventh centuries the Latin interpretive systems available for giving meaning to experience did not proliferate rapidly, nor, allowing for exceptions like Bede or Eriugena, did they attempt to supersede ancient exemplars. But from about 1050 the situation changed radically. An increasing number of hermeneutic models began to compete within the sphere of interpretation, and they were applied with varying degrees of success to an ever-expanding orbit of occurrences. The fit between structures and realities was imperfect: allegory, which initially gave rise to new understanding, also spawned alienation—that is, the feeling that the more one interpreted, the further one got from actualities. Yet the gradual buildup of interpreted experience was one of the chief forces giving continuity to roles, forms of life, and enactments of ideas over time. History was not repeated; it was developed in a genetic unfolding. Models long forgotten—the lives of early medieval saints, legendary Germanic heroes, classical and biblical figures— were revived and made the basis for action. As early as Odo of

Cluny's life of Gerald of Aurillac, which was completed before 942, social and literary norms were beginning to interpenetrate each other so thoroughly as to become indistinguishable. As groups of listeners, readers, and interpreters formed, the inevitable result was the rebirth of textual communities. Here again, the question of oral versus written tradition need not be framed in inflexible terms. What was essential for a textual community, whether large or small, was simply a text, an interpreter, and a public. The text did not have to be written; oral record, memory, and reperformance sufficed. Nor did the public have to be fully lettered. Often, in fact, only the *interpres* had a direct contact with literate culture, and, like the twelfth-century heretic Peter Waldo, memorized and communicated his gospel by word of mouth. Yet whatever the origins, the effects were roughly comparable. Through the text, or, more accurately, through the interpretation of it, individuals who previously had little else in common were united around common goals. Similar social origins comprised a sufficient, but not necessary, condition of participation. The essential bond was forged by means of belief; its cement was faith in the reality of belonging. And these in turn were by-products of a general agreement on the meaning of a text.

From textual communities it was a short step to new rituals of everyday life, whether these were imposed by a monastic rule, a lay confraternity, the search for civic equality, or the ethical values arising from literature itself. It is one of the persistent scholarly myths concerning medieval civilization, fostered by an oversimplified evolutionism, that as literacy and education increased, ritual declined. Certainly a number of rites were on the wane: physical symbolism was replaced by property law; elaborate gift transfers gave way to the market economy; and the sacral element in kingship was balanced by a sense of administrative responsibility. But while such rites deteriorated, another sort of ritual was brought into being and given a social context by groups articulating their self-consciousness for the first time. Heretics, reformers, pilgrims, crusaders, proponents of communes and even university intellectuals began to define the norms of their behavior, to seek meaning and values over time, and to attempt to locate individual experience within larger schemata. Ritual as a consequence did not die; it flourished in a different mode. The rites of a putatively oral society—putative, in fact, since the case is largely argued from silence—began to be looked upon as survivals of an archaic age, while those more closely oriented around a textual presence gained legitimacy and increasingly determined the direction of group action. What Erving Goffman has said about "interaction ritual"[9] in contemporary contexts needed only the additive of texts to become a major force in early modern history.

When men finally got around to writing theories about what they had been doing for some time, such action was inevitably looked upon as a succession of events beginning in the past. In many instances the sequential ordering of the text, the *series verborum* or *narrationis*, was simply and crudely imposed on events in the real world. As a consequence of this interpretive activity, the issue of oral and written communication cannot be separated from that of reform, utopia, and primitivism. Change was presumably brought about to improve things, if not in the short, at least in the long term. As the local, the particular, and the spoken models succeeded to the nonlocal, the universal, and the written, such general notions as mimetic imitation, redemptive typology, and the correct reading of anterior models were inevitably brought to the forefront of the discussion. Utopia, as a result, ceased to be a wholly otherworldly ideal, as it is, for example, in the ninth-century *Vita Anskarii*; instead, it became infused with innerworldly elements, as if, by interiorizing the gospel's message, man could, in Hugh of St. Victor's memorable words, repair some of the damage done in the Garden of Eden and prepare the way for eternal life. Reading and meditation, hitherto largely the private preserves of the monastic life, became, by the later twelfth century, general viatica to perfection. This approach to augmenting self-knowledge of course favored the search after origins or first principles that we associate with primitivism. To be better was to be earlier and to be earlier was to find the ultimate precedent, which, not surprisingly, turned out to be a text. Rapid change, therefore, did not go hand in hand with a decline in religious sensibilities, but, as during the Industrial Revolution, religion adapted to a new context, one that, as it turned out, it had helped to shape.

As the written word gradually worked its way into different areas of life and thought, strategies of interpretation naturally multiplied. Contrary to what synthesizers have proposed, there was no generalized medieval "hermeneutics." Rather there were different, individualistic methodologies adapted to different cultural, psychological, and social needs. How are these approaches to be classified? At the outset of the investigation of any interpretive field, suggests Ricoeur, radical opposites are the best point of departure. "According to one pole, hermeneutics is understood as the manifestation and restoration of a meaning addressed to me in the manner of a message, a proclamation, or as is sometimes said, a kerygma; according to the other pole, it is understood as a demystification, as a reduction of illusion."[10] This distinction, which is another way of stating the functionalist versus formalist hypothesis, can help to classify the medieval interpretive field. But its frame of reference must be altered. In the one case, oral culture does not disappear; it is merely transformed. The interpreter hears a message, as did so many reformers, heretics, and mystics: he or she is motivated by faith and awaits a real or symbolic revelation. In the other, the text's meaning is disguised from the interpreter, who is animated by skepticism, by a suspicion of the given, and by a desire to find the inner truth concealed beneath a dissimulating "integument." During the high Middle Ages these two sets of interests occasionally came into headlong collision and, because they were so hotly disputed within a narrow group of disciplines, influenced each other in a variety of ways. Their conflict lay behind some of the period's most spectacular controversies – Berengar versus Lanfranc, Abelard versus St. Bernard, and, more generally, "monastic" versus "scholastic" notions of the uses of knowledge. Yet despite frequent mutual accusations of "heresy," the rival positions were urged from within what was essentially one hermeneutic environment. While specific interpretations were open to debate, there was less and less questioning of the principle of interpretation through texts. And thus scholasticism eventually overcame its most ardent opponents by forcing them to struggle against it on its own terms.

III

There is a growing recognition that certain developments in medieval thought – not only the interpretive positions but also the theories of language on which they were based – anticipated the contemporary interest in semiotics, structuralism, and hermeneutics. There is much less understanding about where or why such types of thinking arose in the first place. Recourse to ancient exemplars is in this case futile, since the most eloquent statements, such as Plato's *Phaedrus*, were virtually unknown to medieval authors. If one is allowed to simplify somewhat, and to push aside, momentarily at least, the question of cultural diffusion, it can be argued that the medieval state of affairs came about by one of two routes, and that this, in turn, accounts for the dichotomy in the formation of interpretive positions. On the one hand, the literate, exegetical tradition, although occasionally interrupted, never really died. As for oral tradition, it gradually assimilated the written through a process of acculturation; that is, while retaining its explanatory links with the said, the performed, and the physically symbolic, it added *rationes scriptae*, first only as afterthoughts, later as an official record, and finally as a partial displacement of a presumably aboriginal orality. "From the beginning of the contacts with missions," notes a recent observer, "many Melanesians displayed a curiously ritualized (yet practically understandable) attitude towards literacy. They took writing to be merely one more of those inherently ambiguous modes of communication with the supernatural with which they were already familiar."[11] Similarly, in the Western Middle Ages, writing acted as a material representation of speech long before transcription alone could be judged evidence of genuine literacy.

The ambivalence of the medieval reader toward the text is partly revealed in the evolution of the Latin *textus*. The verb *texo*, from which the antecedents of English, German, and Romance language terms for "text" are derived, meant to weave, to plait, or to interlace, and hence, in a subsidiary sense, to compose. The notion of a *series verborum* survives as late as the *Oxford English Dictionary*, which gives as the first meaning of *text*, "the wording of anything written or printed; the structure formed by the words in their order," a notion whose medieval roots were neatly summed up by the lexicographer Calepino when he wrote that *textus* equals *complicatio*, and that *textum* can be defined as "quicquid contexitur aut componitur."[12] From the eleventh century, *textus* began to refer more and more exclusively to the Bible, or more precisely, as Du Cange noted, to the *codex Evangeliorum*; but the dictionary added that the term normally indicated a ceremonial book "decorated lavishly with gold or gems,"[13] which obviously retained its symbolic trappings. Yet the more sophisticated notion of tissue, texture, or style of composition, which may have originated with Quintilian, also survived throughout the Middle Ages, and, to add to the many layers in the idea of a text, never lost touch with its original, tangible associations. Cicero, for instance, in a phrase known to medieval authors, speaks of "tegumenta ... corporum vel texta vel suta"[14] ("the coverings of bodies or weavings or sowings"), and a glossary of late Latin, preserving usages between the second and the sixth centuries, refers to *texta* as connections or chains.[15] Even at the end of the early medieval period, words derived from *texo* dealt more frequently with cloth than with parchment, and the concreteness of the concept lies just beneath the surface of complex notions like Gottfried von Strassburg's *sîn* and Marie de France's *sen*. "The written charm," writes Jack Goody, "is considered to be so effective because it gives speech a concrete embodiment; so can other material objects. . . . But writing clearly has a special value because of its intimate relation to speech."[16] The idea of a text as the material replica of a woven literary composition, whether originating in words or in writing, made perfect sense to a society in which orality still played a large role in cultural communication.

The set of changes we have been discussing may be put in terms that bridge the gap between continental theorists like Saussure and British linguistic philosophers like Austin. Both sides agree that meaning has two essential dimensions, an objective element—what a sentence means—and a subjective element—what a speaker means—although there is much disagreement about each and about their relationship to each other. The rebirth of literacy, it should be stressed, did not bring the objective and subjective dimensions of meaning into existence; it merely threw them into relief in a new way, which, as it turned out, held important consequences for the notion of social action. The objective aspect, which had formerly arisen from a fund of unwritten knowledge more or less shared by all members of the group, became invested in large part in the text, which, being physically apart from the speaker, acquired the same symbolic status as the objects the words had represented and, as time went on, the ontological status previously associated with nature or the divine. The subjective aspect, which had always arisen from the speaker's intentions, remained within the physical bounds of the human voice and the semantic bounds of spoken sentences. But it was now implicated as well in the world of texts—not, of course, limited to the written version of its own statement, but, in a universe of meaning presupposing lexica, glossaries, and the comparison of variants, testable against what Frege calls a proposition's "reference."[17] Abelard, in the well-known preface to the *Sic et Non*, speaks without equivocation on the advantages of a logical and textual reference system, in which the teacher of theology no longer had to cope with the indeterminateness of purely verbal classroom presentation.[18]

How then are we to define a "text" in a medieval setting and to place it on the scale between the objective and subjective aspects of social activity?

To begin, a deficiency must be acknowledged in the medieval manner of conceptualizing the relationship between physical sound and understood sense. Boethius, who is typical of thinking before Abelard, interpreted Aristotle as stating that a written word was an "inscriptio vocis articulatae."[19] A sentence was by implication a written record of spoken sound in meaningful (that is, grammatical) arrangement. In the case of both words and sentences, there was, as noted, a bias toward literate culture as the standard against which the communicability of all discourse was to be measured. By contrast, modern linguistics teaches that speaking and writing are alternative, if interdependent, forms of discourse, and that each contains both objective and subjective elements. In other words, the contemporary assessment is closer to Abelard's view that objectivity cannot be ascribed, as pure realists wished, to intended meaning alone. Yet this was a crucial concession to orality, living experience, and functionalism that the majority of medieval authorities were unwilling to make. For by and large, the latter were convinced that written communication, or its equivalent in speech, was directly reflective of reality, but that purely oral exchange, when it was not backed up by a text, was not. Truth, in other words, was looked upon, as both Augustine and Boethius looked upon it, as an inner essence hidden beneath a textual integument. No such mysteries lay beneath words alone. As a consequence of the formalist bias, medieval theories of how the said, the written, and the understood are interrelated tell us only part of the story of how authors, artists, and philosophers actually viewed relations between language and reality. The other part, to the degree that it can be known, requires postmedieval techniques of analysis.

To take a few examples well known to contemporary discussion: objectivity can be said to exist within the words spoken in two senses, *as* they are spoken and *after* they are spoken, that is, both at the point of enunciation and at the point at which they exist as a message in the hearer's mind. In the oral performance of an epic poem, there is one objectivity in the mind of the singer of tales, which is exteriorized as verse; there is another in the minds of his listeners, which results in part from his words and in part from their understanding; and this, in turn, is partly a group and partly an individual experience. And if the speaker's intentions must be exteriorized to achieve their final meaning, the hearer's understanding comes about by interiorization.

Without as yet referring to written discourse, we may therefore speak of a meaning, as does Abelard, as a conventional agreement between speakers and hearers. The sense they share—which we may call the primal, intersubjective text—is independent of both parties in the exchange. In other words, inasmuch as the speaker's words are rendered meaningful by the use of grammar, syntax, and an agreed sense for words, the text can be said to exist in a putative form even before it is spoken. Without the words spoken (or gestures to replace them), there would be no communication; without the words understood, independently of their having been spoken, there would be no understanding. The text, *qua* inscription, plays a mediating role in both areas: it influences the subjective intentions of the speaker and the subjective intentions of the hearer as well as the presumably objective message they have in common.

But the advent of the text in a permanent form also alters the other relationships in the nexus joining the speaker and the hearer. The significance of the text is obviously no longer identical with the author's intended meaning. If, for instance, we shift from the epic as delivered orally to the epic as read silently and understood, the potential overlap between speaker and meaning disappears. What has up to now been a communication between speaker and hearer in which meaning indirectly involves textual components becomes a process in which texts so to speak play different meaningful games with author, listener, and reader. The speaker, in authoring a text in a written form, gives birth to an autonomous vehicle of exchange; the reader (or hearer, if the text is read to him) receives it as an already coded message, independent of its author but not, it should be noted, of a context, since, at least in part, context is supplied by a common group understanding. The conventional agreement between speaker/author and hearer/reader is still in effect, because speaking and writing, in order to achieve communication, employ the same grammar. And the text, once decontextualized from its original author, together with its social and historical mode of production, can appeal to any audience. The possibility is thereby opened for the consideration of an ontology of the text itself, describing the nature of the reality it represents and the sort of meaning it alone conveys.

As regards literature and society, this development worked in two ways. From about the middle of the eleventh century on, we witness the rise of a literature, first in Latin and later in Old French, that not only sees itself as preserving a record but that, as a set of texts, begins to carry on an interpretive conversation with its own textual past. Also, for the first time in centuries, human relations themselves are seen to behave like texts in possessing both sense and reference.[20] Social organization itself becomes a text worthy of commentary and interpretation.

What was unprecedented in the medieval situation was a new

set of relations between theory and practice as they dealt with the understanding of society. During the early Middle Ages, formalisms predominated: there was one set of rituals reserved almost exclusively for face-to-face encounters using only words and another based upon legal principles using texts. Owing to the widespread rebirth of literacy, especially among the *clerici*, who were inevitably called upon to record transactions, a new reference system for meaningful social action was gradually introduced into a formerly oral network of social relations. Its fundamental tenet was the identification of objectivity with a text. As a consequence of the process of contextualization, questions also began to be asked about the validity of hearsay testimony, oral family record, and collective memory. What became the operative factor in all social discourse was a lexicon or, one should perhaps say, a rhetoric of human behavior, that implicitly adopted a linguistic model based on written language. Even when texts were not present, they influenced intentions, motivations, and psychology as if they were. The oral aspects of exchange could no longer be thought about in isolation; nor could the written ones—which had been subjoined to them, as noted, through acculturation—be considered mere additives to an already existing framework of social organization. In this changing world, there was ever-increasing pressure for a realignment between the oral and the written. Aspects of human relations that were once thought to deal with reality were now considered to deal only with words; hence a literature sprang up, not only glossing and supplementing textually interrelated forms of behavior, but also substituting, as literature, for patterns of life no longer thought to have validity.

Nowhere was this more evident than in the sphere of social record itself. A distinction appeared between what was illustratable through writings and what was not: *antiquitas* emerged as the textual time zone, while *modernitas* was retained for time remembered and related by word of mouth.[21] More significantly, the biological and fictional histories of noble families began to interpenetrate each other in curious ways. Whether one recalled one's genealogy accurately or not largely depended on one's place in the social hierarchy. The best-known example of this phenomenon is a handful of French dynasties in the eleventh and twelfth centuries, whose narrative records all speak of lowly origins in the later ninth or tenth, thereby lending credence to the Romantic notion that this branch of the European feudal nobility was of relatively recent ascendancy. The research of K. F. Werner proved such assumptions to be almost entirely false. In every instance for which witness lists can be found, the French nobility was shown to have descended from Carolingian, if not from Merovingian, ancestors.[22] But the fabrication of lowly origins served social purposes. It justified the closing of noble ranks to a small group, thought to have a common ancestry, while, through the myth of social mobility, it equally justified the effectual climb up the social ladder of many unpropertied *milites*, all aspiring to noble status. It also legitimized gradations within the nobility itself, which was increasingly subjected to the pressures of a money-oriented society in which ancient loyalties could no longer automatically be assumed to hold.

However, above all, such fictive families bore witness to a profound mutation in the nature of kinship itself. Before the tenth century, in such families, there was no sense of lineage, genealogical conscience, or systematic recollection of ancestors. What a lord considered his "family" was a horizontal grouping of individuals, lacking precise consanguineal boundaries. The primary temporal dimension was the present. What really counted was not one's ancestors but one's close associates: it was they who, through the execution of his demands, preserved the local lord's power and, having fulfilled their duties, were appropriately rewarded. In contrast, by the eleventh century the noble individual felt himself constrained by a far more rigid set of kinship ties within his family, all based vertically on agnatic filiation. He was the member of *une race*, whose spiritual capital was transmitted from father to son.[23] He felt noble, Georges Duby adds, because, above all, he was able to claim affiliation with known predecessors—that is, to seek social definition through genealogy.[24] And thus textual models invaded medieval life and thought from another direction.

From the reconstruction of family history, it was a natural step to the interpretable elements in other aspects of past experience, and, from there, to a multitude of applications of hermeneutics to otherwise meaningless events, situations, and relationships. Here again, a few basic forces were at work. Just as, for Aristotle, Abelard, and modern commentators, the study of language, which revolves around signs, must be distinguished from units of discourse, which are based on sentences, so these in turn began to be distinguished from larger units of communication, which were, so to speak, the building blocks out of which temporal and historical consciousness was constructed. As the criteria of literacy were systematically imposed upon cultural developments, they too began to exhibit the characteristics of *langue* and *parole*—that is, an inner linguistic system or code and an outer realm of adaptation or usage. If this had not been the case, the individual participants in collective social activities like the pilgrimage and the crusade, who were, before these group rituals began, presumably not in contact with each other, would have had no common understanding of their action's significance. Evidently, a type of interpretive mechanism was set up that allowed the two sorts of communication, inner and outer, to function at once, with the eventual result, as Paul Alphandéry underlines, that "the crusade, both in its religious context and its power over the collective life, is present in men's minds when the actual crusade begins."[25] Medievalists have been slow to respond to the challenge of such problems. For their part, structuralism and poststructuralist hermeneutics have concentrated rather narrowly on the smaller units of human interchange, such as phonemes, speech acts, and sentences. Where possible, it would be useful to apply a similar sort of analysis to larger idea complexes within the sphere of social and historical action.

IV

In conclusion, it is worth asking why medieval and a good deal of modern thought has avoided discussing these sorts of interconnections. The answer lies in a broader consideration of the issues with which we began.

Throughout the Middle Ages, the study of language was divided into three parts, grammar, logic, and rhetoric. The most important interpretive strategies were either logical or rhetorical, each claiming, although for different ends, an intimate alliance with grammar. More precisely, the function of signs was most often viewed in the context of a relationship between logic and rhetoric. As in the twentieth century, the debate revolved around whether the one or the other had priority.

By and large, logic was preferred. This was true of early medieval approaches to language, which were all Platonic, as well as later ones, which often combined Platonic and Aristotelian influences. (Similar issues found expression in Arab thought, especially in the numerous divisions of the sciences and the inquiries into their epistemological foundations.) Those who looked upon rhetoric as the basis of linguistic communication were usually not academic philosophers but rather what we would today call critical theorists, who commented in a literary, philosophical, or theological fashion on Christian or pagan texts, or who, like Raymond d'Aguilers, had a taste for interpretive history themselves. In short, medieval conceptions of the problem of language and expression exhibited precisely the same tendencies as recent philosophy: there were a majority of thinkers who, like Frege, Husserl, and the early Wittgenstein, gave first place to purely logical considerations, and a minority who, like Heidegger, Derrida, and the later Wittgenstein, criticized inherited logical assumptions and proposed instead an understanding of language in which the meaning of expressions was inseparable from the contexts and conventions that surrounded them.

Within the theory and practice of interpretation in the Middle Ages, a substantial gap gradually opened between the proponents of the logical and rhetorical positions. In many respects each group went its own way, philosophy concerning itself with the issues of logic, language, and metaphysics, and the broader field of interpretation with harmonizing the products of different semantic or semiotic investigations.

There was, however, one central area of recognized disagreement, which, not surprisingly, has also emerged as a center of focus in modern language theory. An important assumption of both Platonic and Aristotelian positions, as well as of grammarians like Priscian, was that the ideas represented by signs were eternal, while the spoken utterances by which we know them were bound by time. For the philosophers, such ideas always stood in a purely logical relationship to each other, no matter how imprecise the forms of expression used to describe them. For the rhetoricians, life, or rather, life informed by texts, was always providing the raw material for new interpretations; and it was experience, rather than presuppositions, to which language was ultimately referred. This experience could be comprised of an actual set of events like the First Crusade, or, as was often the case, a set of events already structured by an existing interpretation, such as the notion of popular election often used to explain the motivation behind the crusade. As a consequence, in the rhetorical strategy, the actual was not invariably understood in terms of the ideal; instead, the acting out, in speech, gesture, or concrete action, gave meaning to the present and, like the sacraments, illuminated words and deeds. To put the matter another way: for the logicians, as for all formalists, there was a radical separation between sense and reference (Frege), or between expression and indication (Husserl), or between surface and deep structure (Chomsky). While they had no equally appealing theoretical structure to put in the place of such notions, the rhetorical school worked within the more manageable realm of tropes, figures, operational definitions, and ad hoc interpretations. For them the world of the text was the world of nature, obedient to natural laws and part of the universe of sense experience by which nature was ultimately known. Headier matters perhaps escaped their attention; but to the degree that they resisted the tendency to universalize merely empirical results and to transform them into new, independent theoretical constructs, they avoided what Wittgenstein accurately called "a general disease of thinking"[26] and set history and theory on a course that ultimately led to an understanding of both literature and society.

CHAPTER THREE

ROMANTIC ATTITUDES AND
ACADEMIC MEDIEVALISM

So far I have argued that the idea of the text offers us a convenient vantage point for demonstrating the linguistic, anthropological, and historical relations between the distant past and the present. One facet of this inquiry concerns the contemporary understanding of the Middle Ages. In chapter 2, I deal briefly with recent attitudes, focusing mainly on the study of language. In this essay I look somewhat beyond the present generation for the origins of popular and academic approaches to the medieval centuries.

I am chiefly concerned with the implications of changes in outlook for overcoming the otherness of the past. I begin by describing the general situation. Then I turn to the solution proposed by a major, bridging figure of the previous period, Erich Auerbach. From the vantage point of his work I attempt to trace the rise, decline, and inevitable resurgence of Romantic postures toward the Middle Ages. Finally I look at the advantages and limitations of postmodernism, which, since World War II, has fragmented the study of the period.

A student of medieval cultural history who also takes an interest in contemporary tastes and values cannot help but be struck by two interrelated changes that have come about since World War II. On the one hand the scientific study of the Middle Ages has made steady progress. Archival, diplomatic, and palaeographical research, together with the computer, the aerial survey, soil analysis, and archaeology, have provided tentative answers to a number of much-debated questions. At the same time a wider set of factors having nothing to do with the professional historian has altered his relation to the less-developed stages of the European past. The appearance of many new nations and the abundant literature on modernization they have generated, despite profound differences from Western evolution, have dramatically heightened the awareness of long-buried patterns of thought and action. Under the influence of the social sciences, history, like the medieval theologian's conception of the deity, has often seemed like a *sphera intelligibilis* whose center is everywhere and circumference nowhere. Yet the results have on the whole been beneficial. Man's psychological distance from the Middle Ages, which was radically increased by industrialization, has to some degree been shortened by the use of techniques and methods of inquiry derived from it. If older bias against the period has not evaporated, it has been subjected to a stronger critical light than ever before. Purged of the worst in Enlightenment and Romantic views, the present age would seem potentially freer from prejudice than any since the seventeenth century, when the serious study of the Middle Ages began.

How has professional medievalism reacted to these possibilities? Paradoxically, by adopting their manner but rejecting their goals. In theoretical discussions it is now commonplace for medievalists to advocate some variety of what Marc Bloch years ago called the comparative method, which in today's language may be described as the union of the synchronic and the diachronic modes of thought. Yet clearly the field is not moving in this direction. Under the beguiling veil of interdisciplinary studies, it is in fact becoming more and more specialized. Leaving aside textbooks, one observes a paucity of large and important theses and a proliferation of minute and specific ones. The books and especially the footnotes are longer, but the subjects invariably more limited in scope. For the academic medievalist, as for the classicist of the last century, the age of bold interpretation would appear to have yielded to that of the cautious advance. Even the social historian is not free from this trend. Although committed to the laudable notion that "l'homme en société constitue l'object final de la recherche historique,"[1] he too often employs statistical methods applicable only to the nonreflective side of man. Confronted with individual experience in art, literature, or philosophy, he falls back on the aprioristic assumptions of *mentalité*.[2] But he is better off than the traditional historian. The latter's "rigorous command of the primary sources, distaste for theory and speculation, and proper aversion to the superficiality which a nodding acquaintance with other disciplines brings in its train"[3] are great strengths. But his resistance to outside influence has canonized a type of empiricism that is best described not as a method but as a theoretical prejudice. It isolated a historian like the late E. H. Kantorowicz, who knew his facts but also maintained that history did not simply consist of mustering them one by one.[4] The gap between *chartisme* and *Annales*, between those who study a document or a period and those who focus on a problem, has been quietly widening since it appeared just before the war. The situation can be summed up as follows: a few writers now devote a good deal of time to articulating their theoretical concerns; the majority go on cultivating their esoteric gardens; and the placid surface of medieval studies remains undisturbed.

In these circumstances, what is called for is not yet another defense of the comparative method—phrases like the sociology of literature and knowledge[5] long ago reached most medievalists' ears—but rather an explanation of why, after constituting a possibility for two generations, it is still so far from being a reality.

I

To begin, it may be instructive to examine the achievement of a universally respected figure whose *theoria* and *practica*, by his own admission, developed throughout the prewar period and crystallized during the conflict.

Erich Auerbach died in 1957. A philologist, he saw matters differently from the general historian, but he had the inestimable advantage of understanding roughly where he stood in the historiography of the Latin Middle Ages. The clearest statement of his aims and methods is found in the introduction to a fragmentary group of essays brought together just before his death.[6] Differing from Karl Vossler, E. R. Curtius, and Leo Spitzer, whose encyclopedic interests he shared and admired, he claimed that his own criticism had shown more opaquely than theirs an awareness of the dramatic changes that were about to take place in attitudes toward the European past. "From an early date," he wrote, "and from then on with increasing urgency, the European possibilities of Romance philology no longer appeared to me only as possibilities, but rather as a task which one could attempt to fulfill for the first time in the present, yet no later than the present."[7] Toward the end of *Mimesis* he had spoken in similar, but less enigmatic, terms. As late as the early years of the century, he had argued, common criteria for organizing and representing reality were shared by a wide variety of European authors. But after World War I political and ideological uncertainty rendered these common assumptions meaningless. In an eclectic universe, authors turned to experiment and innovation in an attempt to present a multifaceted image of reality.[8] In differing degrees the changes in sensibility reverberated through all the arts, not least of all through historical writing itself.

There is no need today to reiterate the personal reasons for Auerbach's sense of urgency; yet neither should they blind one to what is permanent in his work, which, as his own statements make clear, had less to do with them than is often supposed. The circumstances in which *Mimesis* was written have too often taken the place in the reader's imagination of the message it was intended to convey. Of course it is impossible to separate the two completely. Auerbach's later studies were in part a response to the collapse of values and political institutions in his own time. Like many intellectuals in post-Wilhelmine Germany, he felt that a reasonably stable world had willfully surrendered its moral direction and was headed for disaster. But this was not as important an influence on his development as historicism.[9] He caught the movement so close to its demise that the standard studies of it do not as yet mention his contribution. Repudiating the older diplomatic and political variety, as well as the attempts to rescue it in his own time by Ernst Troeltsch and Friedrich Meinecke, he returned to different roots in Vico, whom he first translated for the German public, and to the most incisive non-German critic of Hegelianism, Benedetto Croce. From these two sources and from his broad philological training in the tradition of Philipp August Böckh, he evolved a distinctive aesthetic historicism. Summarizing Vico on one occasion he stated: "Every civilization and every period has its own possibilities of aesthetic perfection. . . . The works of art of the different peoples and periods, as well as their general forms of life, must be understood as products of variable individual conditions, and have to be judged each by its own development, not by absolute rules of beauty and ugliness."[10] He never went too far in urging this position as an end in itself, but rather insisted that it be used to create a counterbalance to rigid canons of genre and style.

Auerbach's method was both a philology and a sociology of literature. Critics on the whole have emphasized what was traditional in his writing; they have had less to say about what was new. In an apparently traditional fashion, he always began with the text. Yet in deliberately dispensing with almost all historical information, he consciously broke with the *explication de texte* as understood in his time. For a parallel, one must look not in literary history but to linguists like Spitzer, who were also experimenting with *Stilistik*.[11] Beginning with the text, Auerbach led the reader immediately into the concrete. He was then able to work outwards from the text as a totality of stylistic relations to the other "forms of life" in the period. "If we assume," he said, "with Vico that every age has its characteristic unity, every text must provide a partial view on the basis of which a synthesis is possible."[12] Despite its arbitrary appearance in his essays, the text was never an isolated phenomenon, and his purpose, unlike Spitzer's, was not to recreate an individual moment or form, but rather, as he put it, to seek out *das Allgemeines*, a universal element that resided neither in laws nor in categories of classification. What was this universal? It was the dialectical relationship between representation and reality, between *Darstellung* and *Wirklichkeit*. Style was the mediator between the two. Using this method Auerbach was not only able to demonstrate the inadequacy of the ancient canons of genre when applied to later periods. By turning tradition on its head, by taking the end point in classical realism as the center of focus, he shed light on the interdependence between experience and expression, the author and the text, and the interpreter, like himself, and the period he was writing about. Thus *Mimesis* was intended to be something more than a contribution to literary criticism; or perhaps he thought that criticism should deal with something more than the purely literary. In this sense, the book may perhaps be viewed as a polite, but firm, reply to the infraliterary and somewhat absolutist *Antike Kunstprosa* of his much-esteemed colleague, Eduard Norden.

How did Auerbach achieve the difficult union of representation and reality, the goal after which in different ways better philosophers like Cassirer and Lukács had vainly striven? Through the simplest of methods: by placing his empirical analyses in a comparative framework explicitly designed to facilitate interpretation. A key concept in this critical transformation is *Ausformung*.[13] As a translation one is tempted to suggest the medieval Latin *ornatus*, amplification, which would capture the Platonic and Wölfflinesque flavor of a term that hovers delicately between literary style and the linearity of the plastic arts.[14] In *Mimesis* the word refers to the filling or modeling out of an inchoate generic type into its specific, fully delineated, sensible form. An identifying detail like Odysseus' scar, he observes, fulfills Homer's stylistic need for the "sensuous amplification of phenomena [*sinnlicher Ausformung der Erscheinungen*]."[15] The basis of Homer's portrayal of the real is "to represent phenomena in a fully delineated way, palpable and visible in their parts, fully defined in their spatial and temporal relations."[16]

The first four chapters of *Mimesis*, which, along with that on Dante, are among the best, present the reader with a carefully chosen set of texts, all of which consciously or unconsciously reflect differing shades of the sensuous, the sensible, the linear—in short, of reality as it "forms itself out." Fortunata struts her stuff at Trimalchio's feast and is immortalized in a few brushstrokes by a parvenu who shares her vulgar tastes but not her good luck. Percennius, inciting a Pannonian legion to insurrection, is cooly dismissed by Tacitus, who sees in history not the interplay of dynamic forces, but only "vices and virtues, successes and mistakes."[17] Ammianus Marcellinus allows the red hair of Peter Valvomeres to pop up for an instant above a mad Roman crowd before squashing it dispassionately into oblivion. The blood feud of Sicharius and Chramnesindus, reflected through the eyes of Gregory of Tours, provides a stylistic mirror for the confusion of the Merovingian age and for the practical spirit that was in the final analysis to bring some order to it. Yet most vivid of all is the scene from the *Confessions* involving Augustine's school friend Alypius. Invited to watch the gladiators by his buddies, he is at first repelled and closes his eyes to avoid the spectacle; but then, irresistibly drawn to the butchery by the shouts of the crowd, he is like the others totally seduced by its horrors. In a single sentence from this scene Augustine sums up the spiritual needs of an age that had abandoned the pragmatic order of the Roman state and in its degradation "reached the stage of a magical and sensory dehumanization":[18] "He looked, cried out, grew excited and carried away with him the madness which would incite him to return, not only with those by whom he was first enticed, but even in advance of them, and what is more, drawing others [Spectavit, clamavit, exarsit, abstulit inde secum insaniam qua stimularetur redire: non tantum cum illis a quibus prius abstractus est, sed etiam prae illis, et alios trahens]."[19]

These are scenes of conflict. At times the struggle is spiritual; more often it is between a legitimized order of authority and those who rightly or wrongly oppose it. Auerbach's concentration on dramatic antithesis perhaps accounts for weaknesses elsewhere in his work, his failure, for instance, dating from his early book on Dante, to fully appreciate allegory.[20] But he never claimed that his view was anything but "partial," and by focusing on situations of conflict he was able, using the single tool of stylistic analysis, to lay bare some fundamental tensions in medieval and modern literature. Again and again he reflects on stylistic disjunction. When he is not describing a mob scene, as in the cases of Percennius and Peter Valvomeres, he focuses on other aspects of the problem, the tension, let us say, in Petronius between the intense subjectivity of the narrator and the supposedly objective situation he is portraying. Yet the most outstanding example of the interplay of popular and learned elements is one to which he devotes only a few lines. In it he saw a "ruthless mixture of everyday reality and the highest and most sublime tragedy"[21] that overthrew the classical rules of style. In *Mimesis* it is illustrated through a single text, Peter's denial of Christ in the gospel of Mark. Taking up a theme he elaborated in detail in his most characteristic essays, "Figura" or "Sermo Humilis," he describes as follows the inner back-and-forth movement by which Peter's denial, reacting back upon his own personality, transforms physical weakness into spiritual strength:

> Peter, whose personal account may be assumed to have been the basis of the story, was a fisherman from Galilee, of humblest background and humblest education. The other participants in the night scene in the court of the High Priest's palace are servant girls and soldiers. From the humdrum existence of his daily life, Peter is called to the most tremendous role. . . .
>
> A tragic figure from such a background, a hero of such weakness, who yet derives the highest force from his very weakness, such a to and fro of the pendulum,[22] is incompatible with the sublime style of classical antique literature. But the nature and the scene of the conflict also fall entirely outside the domain of classical antiquity. Viewed superficially, the thing is a police action and its consequences; it takes place entirely among everyday men and women of the common people; anything of the sort could be thought of in antique terms only as farce or comedy. Yet why is it neither of these? . . . Because it portrays something which neither the poets nor the historians of antiquity ever set out to portray: the birth of a spiritual movement [*die Entstehung einer geistlichen Bewegung*] in the depths of the common people, from within the everyday occurrences of contemporary life.[23]

Passages of such power and insight are rare in the criticism of late and medieval Latin literature. Yet how will Erich Auerbach be remembered best? Not, with rare exceptions, for his studies of individual ideas or authors. Some of his favorite notions, like prefiguration, have become common currency; others, like *sermo humilis*, must be used with caution.[24] Nor are the philological techniques he used, however helpful, any longer fashionable.

But in two areas his achievement was not surpassed in his time. The first was historiographical. *Mimesis* is not only an essay in stylistics; it is also a project in contemporary cultural history. In addition to realism, its subject is the place of the Middle Ages in our own civilization, the manner in which the interpretation of the past is conditioned by the present, and vice versa. Secondly, through his interest in method, Auerbach was able to contribute a number of new problem orientations to medieval literature. These include the study of the reading public as revealed in his early, exciting "La Cour et la ville"[25] and in his last fragmentary paper, "The Western Public and Its Language";[26] his perception of popular elements in medieval Latin and their implications for understanding oral and written tradition; and his belief, now partly reincarnated in semiotics, that the languages of culture are integrative instruments for bringing together group experience and expression.[27] These problems were not new with him, but no other critic of his generation working in the medieval field brought so many of them under one rubric. Nor did any critic make so useful a contribution to general intellectual history. At a time when discussions of medieval literature centered on imagery or individual biography, he attempted to lead the reader back toward the understanding of archetypal conventions. Much historical evidence prior to the twelfth century is in the broadest terms literary in character, and Auerbach, although he deals only with style, suggests ways of uniting these other forms of representation with the real. Like Max Weber, he was a pathbreaker in the interpretive (*verstehende*) sociology of the Latin Middle Ages.

One further insight of Auerbach's must not be overlooked. As regards the interpretation of literature, he felt that he stood at the end of a chain of thinking that went back to Goethe and Schiller. Chapter 1 of *Mimesis* provides some minor footnotes to an exchange of letters between the two founders of German Romanticism, and there is a certain irony that these footnotes were written in Istanbul, where incautious Western ideals traditionally met their antitheses throughout the Middle Ages. Since he wrote, serious realist authors like Tomasi di Lampedusa have appeared, and there have been weak revivals of philology. But neither are in the vanguard of literature or criticism. One is compelled to accept as verified his opinion that his generation of Romance philologists was the last to be able to encompass the Western tradition in a single literary experience. His pessimism was shared by Curtius and Spitzer, and a parallel for the Europocentrism of such critics can be found in the theories of economic development professed by German liberals from Gustav Schmoller on. Long before the war, of course, attention in avant-garde circles had shifted away from the investigation of specific elements in culture and back toward the Enlightenment search for generic laws—so to speak, from difference back toward identity. (The ideological counterpart of this movement, an attempt to repudiate the worst in European narcissism, had as its aim the neutralization of value judgments in art and the legitimization of non-Western traditions.) Auerbach was not opposed to this shift, which he clearly saw was coming, but he tried to draw attention to the other perspective before it disappeared.

II

Auerbach stands out in his generation as a figure who was conscious of a shift in historical perspective and who attempted to reorient his studies to take account of it. But his prophecies, it would appear, have only partly been proven correct. If World War II, *grosso modo*, marked a turning-point in attitudes toward the Middle Ages, then the dominant mode of interpretation should by now be some type of comparison. This is just what it is not. If there is a common denominator in the field, it is a commitment to the medieval period as an organic unity. By their choice of problem and technique, medievalists who claim to be in no way adverse to interpretation nonetheless minimize its potentialities.

Why is this so? The answer lies outside the domain of medieval studies themselves. It arises from a new relationship between popular attitudes toward primitivism, of which medievalism is one, and the institutionalization of the Romantic conception of the medieval epoch. For there are two easily confused ways of defining the Middle Ages, either as a pedagogical notion in the classroom or as a complex myth, a set of subjective responses to the past. Long before the study of the period acquired scholarly respectability, medievalism had exerted a profound influence on many forms of cultural expression. The eighteenth and nineteenth centuries knew radically different versions of the medieval past, and only with the growth of industrialization did it finally cease to function as a mythical substratum operating from below. Although scientific medieval studies had always existed independently of unscholarly fashions in medievalism, the appearance of the field as an area of professional study coincided roughly with the waning of the agrarian way of life in western Europe. Auerbach was fully conscious that the last phases of this development had come to maturity in his own time.

His point of view is not surprising if one reviews a few well-known, but often overlooked facts. The Middle Ages, after all, were invented long before they were studied; they began life with historiographical, not historical, reflection. To the medievals the *media aetas* did not exist at all; it was created by the humanists to describe what they thought they were not, but which in fundamental respects they still were.[28] During the Renaissance, the Middle Ages ceased bit by bit to be a reality people lived without troubling to think about it and began to be a consciously recreated epoch. With the invention of printing, the growth of exploration and the general expansion of the economy, man was to attain the most comprehensive perspective on his past since the Roman Empire. The humanist view, in which history was still united to rhetoric, gradually gave way in the seventeenth century to the scientific study of the medieval West. The two greatest collections of sources, the Bollandist and the Maurist,[29] date from then, as does

the quarrel of the Ancients and the Moderns, out of which grew
the first positive reevaluation of medieval cultural achievement.[30]
Being "half medieval and half modern," figures like Bacon or
Browne were still able to strike a common chord with their medieval background, but perhaps as well incapable of distinguishing
the useful from the otiose in the medieval heritage.[31] With the
Enlightenment, the antiquarian, who studied the Middle Ages
without necessarily imposing a pattern on them, yielded to the
ideologist, who, taking as his primary concern his own place in history, sought in the past a justification and an assurance.[32] And thus
the Middle Ages were reborn as a social myth. As usual, ideology
was fed by ignorance: the Enlighteners had just enough information to form opinions but not enough to make judgments. Typical
was William Robertson, who wrote his history of Charles V without knowing how to read Spanish.

To the Enlightenment, the Middle Ages were primarily a
period; for the Romantics, writing roughly a century later, they
were also a state of mind: and the bridge between the two was
Herder. The Enlighteners, highly conscious of themselves as subjects, made of all past periods mere objects that could be used as
measuring sticks for the present. The Romantics, who wished to
escape from themselves and from the present, began to identify
themselves with the past, to reduce the present, through reminiscence, to cumulative experience, and in doing so to idealize what
the Enlightenment had despised. Herder had taken a middle position between the two extremes. In 1774 he asked: "What right jus-
tifies the arbitrary verdicts of praise and blame which we heap on
all the earth on account of a favorite people of antiquity with
which we have become infatuated?"[33] Such was his comment on
Winckelmann. In contrast to the Enlightenment worship of antiquity, he asserted, like Vico, that every period possessed its own distinctive possibilities of development, that all had contributed

something to human progress. In particular he offered the following reevaluation of the Middle Ages:

> All the books of our Voltaires, Humes, Robertsons and Iselins are, to the delight of their contemporaries, full of beautiful accounts of how the enlightenment and improvement of the world, philosophy and order emerged from the bleaker epochs of theism and spiritual despotism. All this is both true and untrue. . . .
>
> Often in these apparently coercive institutions and corporations there was something solid, cohesive, noble and majestic, which we certainly do not feel, nor are scarcely able to feel, with our refined ways, disbanded guilds yet shackled states, and with our innate cleverness and all-embracing cosmopolitanism. . . . You praise nothing so much as the breaking of these ties and know of no greater good which ever happened to mankind than when Europe, and with it the world, became free. Became free? What wishful thinking! If only it were true! If only you could realize what these earlier circumstances . . . did in fact achieve: Europe was populated and built up; generations and families, master and servant, king and subject, interacted more strongly and closely with one another; what one is wont to call "simple country seats" prevented the luxuriant, unhealthy growth of the cities, those slagheaps of human vitality and energy, whilst the lack of trade and sophistication prevented ostentation and the loss of human simplicity in such things as sex and marriage, thrift and diligence, and family life generally. The mediaeval guilds and baronies engendered pride in the knights and craftsmen, self-confidence, steadfastness and manliness in their spheres of activity, and checked the worst torment of mankind, the enslavement of lands and souls under a yoke which now apparently, since the earlier social enclaves have been disbanded, everyone accepts readily and wholeheartedly.[34]

As the early, literary phase of Romanticism developed into a broader cultural movement, this humane (and yet inaccurate) perspective was lost. The Romantic ideology became as hardened as the Enlightenment opinions it had rejected. As early as Rousseau, the primitive aspect of the Middle Ages had begun to take the shape of a new myth. The distance the Enlighteners had placed between themselves and the Middle Ages was transformed into an equally self-conscious identification. As industrialization gradually affected larger and larger groups of people, whole segments of medieval utopian thinking were rudely revived and pressed into service. The Middle Ages began to be associated with a lost state of innocence: for the moralist, they were paradise without sin; for the socialists, without private property.

Friedrich Meinecke, commenting on Herder's mature view of the Middle Ages, points out that it was the turning-point not only in his own philosophical development but in the general evolution of historicism.[35] But Meinecke did not consider the opposite possibility—namely, that without the Middle Ages to reflect upon, historicism might not have been conceivable at all. For this belief demanded an unusual stance on the part of the interpreter of the past, a simultaneous distance and nearness, which was, by the very nature of things, easier for a northern European to achieve with respect to the medieval than to the ancient world. The Romantic historicists wanted to have their cake and to eat it; to retain the Enlightenment notion of the Middle Ages as a distant and objective period, but at the same time to bring that period near at hand, to add their subjective responses to it. There is a fundamental tension in Romantic approaches between the desire to make the Middle Ages an entity and to interpret them. In Marx, who is in this respect fully characteristic, feudalism is both an earlier state of history and a more humane economic system than capitalism.[36] Yet with all their faults, Romantic attitudes were an improvement on the eighteenth century. If at times they prettified chivalry or ennobled monastic otherworldliness, they nonetheless deepened historical understanding through careful factual research. The Middle Ages, Meinecke notes, were no longer an "untrimmed block of stone, which had to be rounded and smoothed off by the art of the moderns."[37] Their distinctive contours were now appreciated for what they were. Even in the phase of romantic activity that followed the Napoleonic Wars, when so much English and French medievalism was a thinly disguised veil against political radicalism, many concrete advances were made: collections of music and folklore, critical editions of major figures like Dante, Chaucer, and Villon, the serious study of medieval genres like the lyric and the *chanson de geste*, and the beginnings of the rehabilitation of medieval scientific thought. The bad came with the good, the bogus medievalism of the Victorian church along with Ruskin and Viollet le Duc.

Despite the dramatic contrasts in popular attitudes toward the Middle Ages in the eighteenth and nineteenth centuries, a slow but steady progress was made in illuminating the darker corners of the period. In the *Monumenta Germaniae Historica*, launched in 1818, and the École des Chartres, in 1821, the work of Mabillon and Montfaucon was furthered by scholars of the caliber of Waitz and Delisle.[38] Yet even allowing for such continuities, scholarly medievalism was only a minor tributary of wider cultural fashions, and inevitably, if indirectly, reflected their changes. For the brief recapitulation of these mutations one need look no further than the differing opinions on how an early text ought to be edited. One school, descending from Lachmann via Bentley, held that as correct a version as possible should be reconstructed by a deductive utilization of the best witnesses. Another school, whose chief advocate much later was Bédier, maintained that for vernacular texts in particular the process of reduction to a single archetype could misrepresent the book available to the original readers.[39] The aim of editing, others added, was not only to provide a legible text but also to recreate its linguistic and historical context. Clearly these two positions have their roots in the Enlightenment and Romanticism. In Lachmann's view, the distance between the Middle Ages and modernity is emphasized by the editor's conscious reconstitution of the text; in Bédier's, the nearness, by his activity as a passive mir-

ror for both text and context. A part of the contemporary disagreement in the field arises from the different problems of ancient versus medieval works. But it also results from inheriting two distinct
traditions. The good editor still wishes in part to emulate the
Enlightenment goal that history, in revealing the perversities of the
past, will free him from them. But he is also tainted by historicism.
His recreation of context, if only in the apparatus, may be interpreted as a minor tributary of relativism, and his search for origins
and analogies implies a characteristically Romantic conception of
the organic unity of an age.[40]

The general historian faces these two traditions in a more sophisticated form, and his reluctance to define a mode of interpretation
results in part from his failure to realize that both have reached a
dead end in his own time. As long as the pedagogical apparatus of
historicism was intact and as long as authors and artists who had
personally participated in the last phases of Romanticism were
alive, the Middle Ages could derive their existence from a broader
emotional commitment to the past. That is to say, the Middle
Ages, which did not exist for the medievals, and which had for
three centuries drawn their historical vitality not from accumu-
lated scholarly research but from their status in a group of culturally conditioned responses, were able to maintain their frail
existence as long as the structure of belief that had brought them
into being was still intact. But after World War II, when so many
of the institutions and authors that had kept Romantic ideas alive
had passed from the scene, and when figures with so comprehensive a view of literary history as Curtius and Auerbach could only
speak of "the Western tradition" in the past tense, it could not be
helped that the Middle Ages, as a foundation on which cultural
myths had been erected, should begin to show signs of old age.
This is just what happened. The foundation, now lacking repairs
and in some cases its former tenants, started to decay. In the context of postwar culture, the Middle Ages could no longer be said to

exist as they had for the Enlighteners and the Romantics. Old battles, the symbolic gestures of the academy, continued to bloody the landscape: Catholic and Protestant views of Christianity, Marxist and liberal approaches to feudalism, Romance and Germanic interpretations of legal history. But this was largely shadowboxing. Once the Middle Ages were no longer an objectified period or a subjective state of mind, such controversies, if scholars had let them, could quietly have faded into irrelevance. That they did not can best be attributed to the instinct for survival in postwar academic medievalism.

In suggesting that after World War II the Middle Ages, as a set of subjective attitudes toward the past, had lost the greater part of their raison d'être, one is only adding a conclusion to what was considered logical thinking for three centuries. The Renaissance invented the Middle Ages in order to define itself; the Enlightenment perpetuated them in order to admire itself; and the Romantics revived them in order to escape from themselves. In their widest ramifications "the Middle Ages" thus constitute one of the most prevalent cultural myths of the modern world. Nor has this myth ever been subjected to very acute analysis. Each era since the Renaissance has seen its distinctive histories of the period. But is there a thorough study of the Middle Ages in history? Moreover, such a postmortem would not have been desirable much before the conflict. For there had been many dissenters from the accepted orthodoxy of medievalism—Marc Bloch, because he was a martyr, is only the best known—but almost no one listened to them. The economic and sociological wing of later historicism, typified by Otto Hintze, had long held out the possibility of freeing it from value-laden categories.[41] Neogrammarians like Meyer-Lübke had just as actively opposed philology.[42] The Russian formalist movement, initiated by medievalists, among others, was healthily ahistorical.[43] Anthropology, originally indebted to Henry Maine's medieval classifications of social relations, soon rejected them, but medievalists paid no attention. Even the game theory of culture proposed by Huizinga, which took steps toward breaking down periodizations, had no successors. Before World War II, those who felt that the historiography of the Middle Ages was undergoing significant changes were an insignificant minority. Mental structures so deeply entangled with historical cobwebs had to be destroyed from the outside. Above all, before the Middle Ages could be abandoned as myth, Westerners had to give up the idea that Europe was the standard against which all other cultures were to be measured. The moral and physical conflagration of World War II did just this. Ideas that had lost their creative vigor, and that clung to the educational system like parasites, were destroyed along with their benefactors. Erich Auerbach typified those whom political circumstances forced to articulate positions that in more stable times might have remained unexamined.

III

To summarize: historians have generally assumed that the Enlightenment and Romanticism gave birth to differing conceptions of the Middle Ages. But this view from above makes the assumption that history is a one-way street. It would be equally valid, if less popular, to suggest that the surviving medieval institutional structure, which in no sense gave rise to these movements, nonetheless interpenetrated every level of their development. The Middle Ages, after all, do not end abruptly when historical perspective shifts in the Renaissance. In a tattered form, elements of them survive the sixteenth and seventeenth centuries, even, it may be argued, the final breakup of the feudal monopoly of the soil symbolized by 1789. The real turning-point is industrialization. Nor do the Middle Ages emerge as a period in the nineteenth century simply because history had at last become a university discipline, but rather because universities, together with other supporters of museum culture, had begun to perpetuate *per monumenta* what was finally ceasing to exist *in vita*. Thus there was a somewhat delayed relationship between the progressive disappearance of medieval institutions and the gradual institutionalization of academic medievalism. Eric Hobsbawm notes: "In Lancashire we can observe the ancient ways of spending holidays—the rush bearing, wrestling matches, cock-fighting and bull baiting—dying out after 1840; and the forties also mark the end of the era when folksong remained the major musical idiom of industrial workers."[44] Similar phenomena could be found in other parts of Europe, and in each case the principle was the same. Phoenixlike, cultural articulation was reborn in its own ashes: the museum was erected where the actors had once stood.

The contemporary predicament of medieval studies arises from a new relationship between these hitherto conflicting forces. Throughout the vicissitudes of its development, the historiography of the medieval Latin West not only obeyed the broader laws of sociocultural change; as both subject and object in its universe of reflection, it also exerted a strong influence on their direction. But this is precisely where the present age differs. In the comparative method it has a problem orientation more subtle than those of the Enlighteners or the Romantics. But the organization of medieval studies ensures that those to whom the opportunities of that method are being extended are among the least likely to take them up. The reason is that academic medievalism no longer needs to pay much attention to wider cultural change. There are societies to guarantee its institutional survival and an audience of professionals to read its specialized publications. As a consequence, the comparative method remains a door that many have opened but through which few have passed.

Societies for the study of the Middle Ages are reasonably strong in both Europe and North America. But there have been few sustained efforts at bridging the gap between academic medievalism and general culture. One such effort was neo-Thomism, led by Jacques Maritain and Etienne Gilson. The movement has done a great deal for the study of medieval philosophy, but it has also had the limitation of being oriented around a single university discipline. Another complex of ideas has crystallized around the notion of periodic renaissances in the Middle Ages. This has had the advantage of offering a modernist image of a historical period that has often acted as a repository for religious and political antimodernism. The renaissance idea owes its inception largely to Charles Homer Haskins, whose dazzling gifts and magnetic personality dominated medieval studies in his generation in America. Haskins' most influential and popular book is *The Renaissance of the Twelfth Century*, first published in 1927. The complicated intellectual origins of this volume have never been fully sorted out. Something like a quarter of it is devoted to his own speciality, Latin translations from Greek and Arabic originals during the period of revival. But there are other forces at play: among the problems, Haskins' account of secular revival says little about Europe's most profound religious upheaval before the Reformation.

It is tempting to speculate that Haskins' model of twelfth-century Europe was built in the image of the America that he knew. Whether or not this was actually the case, he provided a view of the period in which his fellow citizens could take comfort. His is an optimistic story of triumph: Europe emerges from localism, superstition, and administrative chaos into law, order, and strong central government. To those who admired the frontier, he offered the parallel of Norman expansion and new cultural horizons. To those who saw themselves passing from otherworldly asceticism to material plenty, he offered an earlier paradigm of technical and scientific progress that had practical results. To recent immigrants weary of disparaging comparisons between their chosen land and Europe, he presented a version of European history that appeared to follow the doctrines that had founded the New World.

It is always easy to criticize a historiography that has lost novelty's charm. Haskins' optimism nowadays seems somewhat naive. A recent survey of the principles behind the twelfth-century renaissance has left his basic thesis intact, but has dramatically broadened its compass of interests. One of the guiding ideas behind the shift in mentality is the replacement of the notion of renaissance with some combination of renewal and reform. But there has also been a strong influence from methods outside the field of medieval studies and from the study of societies with medieval features elsewhere in the world. This has resulted in the blending of conceptualizations from within European history, such as renaissance, with the comparative focus of anthropology, quantification, and decentering literary strategies.

No one knows why these types of comparison appear desirable today or why, despite their obviousness to some, they were unacceptable previously. The reasons usually advanced, such as decolonialization, the communications revolution, Marxist analyses of the superstructure, or even the progress of medieval studies, all have an arbitrary ring to them. But there can be no doubt that the present age, as Auerbach suggested, is one of reevaluation, and that the watershed was World War II. Moreover, just as the new insights are coming from outside traditional medievalism, resistance is coming from within. The nervousness is understandable. Of all the historical periods that entered the university curriculum in the nineteenth century, the medieval was the most benighted with prejudice and false hopes. It had to work much harder than its cousin, classical studies, to become established. In my view, a price was paid. Romantic attitudes are still alive and well in some circles. Worse, the Middle Ages continue to be a refuge for religious archaism and political reaction. The ideological battering that medieval studies took in the past offers no real justification for the perpetuation of inflexible attitudes in the present. It is one thing for a group to assert its right to exist, quite another for it to maintain that its existence guarantees its relevance.

But the uncritical support of a comparative method also holds great dangers. It is, after all, only a possibility, not a panacea: a method of inquiry, not a substitution for facts. Its very obviousness presents an opportunity and poses a threat. The novelty is the unrealized potential of a subjective problem orientation; the threat is the historian's incapacity to perceive its subjectivity. The Enlightenment and Romanticism, as distinctive periods of reflection on the Middle Ages, both mistook their subjective responses to the past for the purported object to which they were responding. The present age is no less ideological than previous ones; it may even be more so. Therefore one presumes that a similar danger persists. But in a time of reassessment, ideology is a necessary evil. The Romantics could never have escaped the grasp of the Enlighteners by the use of reason alone. They needed myth and commitment, which are polite terms for ideology. Today the situation is no different. Those who are urging the comparative framework most loudly are in politicized fields like semiotics and poststructuralism. Their goal may well be to add to the store of knowledge, but their contemporary relevance derives mainly from telling their adepts what they want to hear. They are indeed rejecting old myths, but they are also creating new ones. Like all mythmakers, they hold out a new unmoved mover around which all other constellations of ideas must revolve. The historian, in particular the medievalist, must choose between getting on with his work and becoming a religious devotee. On the rarest of occasions he may combine his respect for the facts with a genuinely new interpretation. Such was the case of Erich Auerbach, who humbly offered *Mimesis* to those who had kept faith in another age of tempestuous ideology in values that now seem emptied of meaning.

CHAPTER FOUR

LITERARY DISCOURSE AND THE SOCIAL HISTORIAN

The relationship of literary scholarship to the writing of history is always problematic. Granted that critics and chroniclers are both focused on a reality of sorts, their approaches nonetheless differ. In part, this is attributable to the type of material they are writing about. But mostly it is a question of professional allegiances and their hidden ideologies, as well as unstated notions about what is or is not considered respectable knowledge in each discipline. In chapter 1, I take an optimistic view of recent developments that favor close cooperation between the two fields. In chapters 2 and 3, I examine the potential benefits, both theoretical and practical, within one time frame, the Middle Ages.

In this essay I attempt to explain why this mutual enrichment has not come about sooner, and why it does not yet interest a great many students of literature or history. I look first at the presumptions of historians faced with the challenge of social sciences whose claim to intellectual rigor is a source of both inspiration and frustration. Then I consider the paradoxical situation of literary theory, one of the century's growth industries in university life. My argument is that the rise in types of interpretation has not been satisfactorily matched by an opening up to extraliterary issues. Excepting the field of deconstruction, the new strength of literary criticism has not resulted in self-examination within the discipline. From within history and the study of literature the foundations of a joint structure have been laid, but the edifice itself has never been built. The question is, why not?

I

Let me begin with a statement in which representatives of these disciplines can find some common ground. In any community or period of time, two sorts of change are presumably always going on at once. There is real change, which is happening but may not be perceived, and there is perceived change, which may or may not be taking place.

Historical writing is largely the story of perceived change. Change in an objective sense may well be taking place, but the materials out of which books on history are made never reflect it directly. Instead, they tell the story of various, partial recordings of change. However these are disguised they really add up to interpretations.[1] Even quantitative history, the most ambitious of recent objectifying techniques, does not provide a satisfactory account of transformations in the external world. I do not wish to argue that *esse* equals *percipi*, or that pure objectivity, like subjectivity, is indescribable. These are problems for philosophy. I merely contend that, for the historian engaged in the everyday practice of his craft, objectivity and subjectivity exist in a rough continuum. Drawing a hard-and-fast line between them is impossible. The historian tries to use the evidence in such a way that his bias or that of the original participants is balanced by countervailing forces, to which he often attempts to give an air of theoretical respectability. But in the last analysis his approach boils down to common sense.

Looking back over historical writing since the nineteenth century, one finds two goals repeatedly stated. There is a demand for a closer accounting for change in the external world. At the same time there is an awakening to patterns of inner development. Rightly or wrongly, the difference between these two orientations has been viewed popularly as a contrast between objectivity and subjectivity. About a century ago, economic history emerged from legal and political history as the most faithful adherent of the external-world hypothesis. In the twentieth century, especially since World War I, social history has incorporated economic history into a larger and more flexible framework—the social system of which economy is a part—while retaining something of its rigor of method. The link between the two is provided by new methods of counting, which also furnish the theoretical justification for retaining the empirical framework. No one doubts that quantification is a good thing. But its success is relative, not absolute. Those who entertain the wildest illusions about statistical methods understand little about the limits of mathematics. Professionals are less ecstatic.[2]

The mature view is that the problem of objectivity and subjectivity has not disappeared. It has merely been translated into a language that most humanistic scholars do not understand. One way of throwing the issues into relief is to point out that the question is an old one. It goes back to the beginnings of modern historical thought. There is not much in the contemporary debate on the methods and goals of history that was not foreshadowed in the seminal exchange of views that took place between Ranke and Burckhardt. As Hans Liebeschütz remarks in a perceptive essay, Ranke's "optimistic belief in the permanence of an order . . . and in the lasting harmony of political power, peaceful prosperity and cultural development, appears almost shallow by comparison with the outline of things to come drawn with uncanny perspicacity in the private letters which Burckhardt . . . wrote at the same period. There is a striking contrast between the penetrating pessimism of the remote observer in Bâle and the deceptive feeling of unshakable security in the mind of the Berlin scholar."[3] The historical world is still divided into optimists and pessimists. But they are no longer speaking to each other in a common language.

That is why there are fewer areas of agreement than there might be between empirical historians and students of literature. The passing of a century has brought about neither marriage nor divorce but rather, after the fashion of medieval romance, endless extensions of an increasingly frustrating courtship. To some historians, all literary statements, including literature in the normal sense as well as laws, contracts, and other records, contain varying degrees of subjectivity. They are formed before the historian reforms them. Other writers have rediscovered narrative discourse, and look upon this primary shaping as an advantage. But this is not the general rule. As it acquired respectability, social history rejected impressions in favor of what could be measured. Most social historians still use literary sources for providing illustrations of what is more precisely demonstrable from evidence uncontaminated by human reflection, or so they think.

The statistically oriented social history that was born from economics toward the end of the last century was a great improvement on what dominated the field before. But its success created new problems. Literary critics propose that texts must be analysed within a system of purely linguistic or semantic relations, rather than with reference to events in the outside world. Somewhat ironically, many historians would agree, not because they wish to restore the integrity of the text but in order to exclude the problematical literary element from their field of endeavor. The science of one group thereby becomes the superstition of another. Among the minority of historians who regard theory as an aid to understanding the past, there is no generally accepted way of dealing with subjective materials, even if they are eminently worthwhile. Often they are looked upon as radioactive, and avoided.

The incapacity of students of social history and literature to communicate better is to some degree the fault of philosophy. In particular, it results from the failure of phenomenology to move in the direction of social reality and the failure of the sociology of knowledge to move away from it. Husserl had no successors who were not as programmatically inclined as he was. The sociology of knowledge, however widely it has influenced historical writing, remains a suggestive hypothesis, not a method, even in its most widely accepted form, the *mentalité* theory developed in *Annales*. The by-products of each movement have been very valuable. Through phenomenology, everyday experience has been taken from the post-Cartesian hinterland and given a place of importance in the analysis of social reality.[4] The sociology of knowledge, which was pioneered by Marx and Max Weber, has left in its wake the largest historical thesis of the century, the debate on the origins of capitalism and modernization. Yet, leaving aside newer approaches like semiology, which cannot yet be adequately judged, it would seem to a practicing historian that the various groups interested in a theoretical discussion of ideas and society—which include anthropologists, sociologists, linguists, and nonanalytic philosophers—are farther apart than ever before.[5]

The two intellectual strategies mentioned also appear to be reviving a modern equivalent of the medieval discussion of realism and nominalism—that is, the question of whether concepts have an existence independent of individuals or whether they are just generalizations based on them. All those who believe that cultural phenomena are superstructures of the economic relations governing production in society are nominalistic, since, for them, culture exists *post rem*. On the other side are phenomenologists and realists, who reject all forms of reductionism and insist that cultural phenomena, existing *ante rem*, can only be considered meaningful to the degree that they relate to each other.

Nominalism is superficially attractive to the social historian because it allows at once for the succession of economic, social, and cultural life and for an analysis based on allegedly objective factors, the conflicts and convergences that create the superstructure in the first place. This position also appears to echo theory formation in hard sciences like physics. But this point of view is flawed. It is widely acknowledged among sociologists of knowledge familiar with language philosophy that no kind of cultural entity can be reduced to its supposedly preexisting parts without transforming a repository of meaning with many dimensions into discrete pieces of information that can only answer restricted questions yes or no. A more sensible approach lies in the other direction.

For, if it is theoretically less precise, it has two advantages from the outset. It recognizes the autonomy of culture,[6] and it questions some commonly held assumptions about the nature of a historical event. The historian in the positivistic tradition assumes that event is related to fact rather than to relation—that is, to an assumed objective reality, not to a system of interdependent factors, some subjective, some objective. As a result, a text, even one that treats events alone, cannot itself be an event: it is something that is derived from real or imagined events. The obvious problem with this approach is that events assumed to have taken place objectively only occupy a meaningful position in a "history" to the degree that they are perceived, either by the original participants, by the later historians, or, potentially at least, by a series of intervening interpreters. In other words, they have been subjectivized. They are not as subjective as a text of pure fiction created for an occasion, but have more in common with such a narrative than with the event-structure of the external world. Let us not be deceived by the skepticism of much historical writing, that arid criticism of documents that pretends to take the reader behind their rhetorical facades and into a world of sober facts. Historical writing does not treat reality; it treats the interpreter's relation to it. For an event does not stand alone as an isolated object of thought, except by abstraction. It can only be understood as one element in a narrative that is stated or implied. To rephrase the two positions of which I speak above, an event can be understood as the product of something or as the intention to be something. As a product, it is the consequence of earlier, but not necessarily related, events—such as, for example, the *consuetudo* that appears as "law" in the medieval manor after emerging from a welter of customary practices. As intention, it is related to thoughts and actions that will take place but have not yet done so, and it derives its meaning from someone's looking back from the vantage point of a later time—as, for example, when the same feudal *consuetudo* is considered a "law" by medieval commentators or modern historians. Literary critics may unwittingly contribute to the view of an event as an isolated object by artificially separating texts from their contexts—that is, by considering the text not as it comes into being in the reader's mind, nor as he reacts to it, but only as something in itself, the totality of whose meaning is assumed to arise automatically out of some inner, objective life. But the text, too, is a complex event.

It is also an arbitrary one. For every text is a literary individual. Historians, who readily grant "uniqueness" to events, are not always willing to make the same concession for texts. At best, they are willing to allow that a text is independent in a negative sense. For the complex inner structure of a text is difficult to assimilate into a picture of reality that is built up slowly and patiently from a mass of details verified from other texts. The historian is mainly interested in producing a picture that is coherent by a process of text-formation. The already-produced text, which results from a similar development in the past, cannot contribute in the same way again to creating pastness. It would have to be taken apart to show how its strategies of persuasion contribute to this illusion, for which the completed text, as a monument, acts as a witness and a guide. To many historians, the arbitrariness of this type of birth is unacceptable.

Why is this so? One reason is that it places an uncomfortable burden on authorship. Authors, whose will and craftsmanship bring texts into being, have a hegemony over their materials, just as, in earlier times, an all-powerful deity was thought to have authored the universe. Playing the part of divinities bothers historians because it challenges the scientific ideology that lies behind the facade of accurate, impersonal research. They do not want to see themselves as moral authorities.

But neither do they wish to be seen as believing naively that they are face to face with reality. The external-world hypothesis normally appears in a modified form in which traditional authority is shifted away from the author as creator to the material as shaper of the text. Therefore, while the ultimate knowability of reality is abandoned, the ideological certainty associated with it is retained. The final goal may be out of reach, we are told, but the quest is worthwhile. In any event, it is the best thing we can do in the circumstances. Philosophically speaking, there may be no objectivity for the historian to hang on to. But that does not mean he or she has to give up the stance that sees one's authoring as a subjective activity. For this is another way of stating one's commitment to objectively representing the past.

But, in this case, the real commitment is not to explanation, but to order, coherence, and hardware. One effectively bypasses a lasting achievement of nineteenth-century historical writing, the demonstration that meaning arises from history's changing capacity for reflection. The problem is not how, or where, one gets evidence, but how it adds up. The choice for the historian is to remain locked within a system in the name of regularity and repetition, and merely to assemble texts out of facts, or to move into the realm of signification. If this is done, then the theoretical issue of text-formation cannot be put off indefinitely. The historian cannot take refuge in inductive methods. He has to assume that, in making history, he is also thinking, explaining, and interpreting, and that the primary tool for this activity is writing. He, the facts, and the texts are part of a single process. He is not an innocent bystander. The most serious limitation of the external-world hypothesis is not theoretical, since few historians have the time or intellectual equipment to make a thorough examination of their assumptions. It is practical. Owing to the uneven survival of the sources for writing history, the problem is especially acute for the classicist, the medievalist, and the early modernist. In the ancient world there are few regularly recurring series of documents. Almost everything one reads is literary. In the Middle Ages, outside England and Italy, there is no continuity in sources before the twelfth century. Even then, their regional distribution remains exasperating down to the fourteenth century, when European archives and libraries begin to provide large amounts of data. If one is writing history outside Europe, the situation is normally worse. Many of the written traditions of formerly colonial countries were not set up before the eighteenth century. Oral cultures of Asia and Africa have histories that antedate those of Europe, but we know virtually nothing about them until the first European visitors provide us with quaint descriptions and travelers' accounts.

If one is to accept the positivistic thesis, even as a rough guide, there can be no social history before the time of large-scale production of data and figures. In other words, by an ironic quirk of historical conscience, one must begin writing "social" history from a date by which many of the fundamental institutions of Western and Eastern society had completed their formative stages of growth. Although the gaps in statistical information are slowly filled in the centuries that follow, the problem is not on that account any easier to solve. It is merely obscured. For, from the fourteenth century in Europe, and from a variety of dates elsewhere, there have been two parallel, but different, experiences of change. One is put together by the historian from archival sources; the other has been assembled in more schematic units through the conscious work of the actors themselves. Instead of exploiting the advantages of this situation, the historian usually regards it as a nuisance. Very often an attempt is made to reduce the cultural material to the common denominator of the statistical; or, what is worse, the statistical method is employed for charting changes in *mentalité*, as if men's minds could be lumped together like land transactions.

It is not my purpose to inquire deeply into the reasons why a position rejected so long ago by leading thinkers has persisted among economic and social historians. But doubtless, as the basis of this idea lies a "real world" that has parallels with the type of reality posited in classical physics before Einstein. This world is not visible, but it is knowable through induction. It is in this sense that history can claim to be reasonable and rational. Historical writing is thus an apologetic whose moral is coherence.

For the author is saying, as he did when the discipline was a branch of theology, that a reasonable model in the past can be contrasted with the irrationality of the present. By this type of argument, one can reduce all non-European cultures to subcultures, and all products of the unconscious to aspects of conscious experience. All symbolic heresies, they are just deviants of an established conceptual church. It matters little if dialectical reason is substituted for reason, since it too, when placed outside the realm of investigable experience, becomes an unchanging, transcendental point of reference. Lévi-Strauss attacked the notion that there is any easy formula for equating history and humanism.[7] But his "history" is something of a straw man. What has happened to historical writing since the high peaks of the nineteenth century may be a disappointing story, but the main protagonist is not recalcitrant humanism. It is the flat landscape. As meaning has gradually been pushed into the background, it has been taken up by disciplines less self-conscious about engaging in reflection, not only literary studies, but interpretive linguistics, philosophy, and anthropology.

At this point some examples may be useful. I draw them from the Middle Ages, the period most familiar to me. But the remoteness from more recent times should not obscure the general issues. Take the miracle. Counting the number can be instructive, especially if sex and generational differences, geographical distribution, and the frequency of psychological irregularities are also recorded. But these factors are exogenous. The miracle, we may argue, really falls outside the boundaries of empirical social history. For although embedded in social reality, the miracle is not itself a social fact—in all probability, it did not take place.

This sort of reasoning, however, only confuses the understanding of a many-sided phenomenon by imposing a bogus scientism on it. The point is not whether a miracle "took place," but that people whose social affiliations can be the object of empirical study have explained an aspect of their behavior in terms of it. These behavioral patterns in turn link up with others. The miracle is a catalyst that focuses the attention of the original actors or the later observers on the stresses and accommodations within the social system as a whole.

One can take a similar line of attack with witchcraft, heresy, games, tournaments, carnivals, the devil, and rites of birth, maturity, and death. The shifting boundaries between real men are sometimes best observed from the vantage point of an agreed psychological boundary that shifts. At the other end of the spectrum, even the basic changes in social structure can be distorted by paying attention only to so-called objective changes. Take the fundamental problem of freedom and slavery, around which, Marc Bloch maintained, all later questions of medieval social organization revolved.[8] In the Carolingian period the juridic status of the free man and the slave were clearly delimited, but within fifty years of Charlemagne's death in 814, a new social framework was beginning to make its appearance. Yet the older categories, *liber* and *servus*, far from falling immediately out of use, continued to be employed. They can be described as archaic survivals of a previous age; but they were also instruments deliberately used for regulating day-to-day relations between men and women. The naive social historian, however, limits the analysis to the frontier of new normative relations, where real changes are thought to be taking place. Older terminology is dismissed, or treated merely as a backdrop.

But this is to pledge oneself to an orthodoxy of popular Romanticism: namely, to witness, not change and continuity, but change alone. The explanation of change is nothing more than a description of a perception of change. And this introduces a new imbalance into what is being said. As far as freedom and slavery are concerned, action and reflection did not coincide. It took social psychology well over a century to catch up with gradually changing realities. Only around 1100 did men begin to invent an adequately flexible vocabulary for expressing their ideas about liberty in society. Increasingly, they demanded to participate as individuals in civic and religious affairs, and they began to enrich the epic and feudal literary codes with a secular moral and ethical structure. Throughout the long period of adjustment all classes of people, both rich and poor, continued to look upon the older formulae as part and parcel of the social reality they experienced.[9] Such categories formed a part of their conscious relation to a past in which the present was enveloped and dissolved as an independent mode of perception.

In areas like these, social reality is an intermingling of reality and perceptions. The two cannot be separated. But, if that is the case, what sort of reality is this? First of all, it is a whole reality, not one artificially divided into object and subject by the demands of specific strategies of narration. It assumes that historical evidence differs in degree, not in kind, and that the impartial observer is best understood as a necessary fiction in historical storytelling. With impartiality eliminated, the possibility of an aprioristic phenomenology or sociology of knowledge also disappears. What remains for the historian to deal with is simply the multidimensionality of change, which it is his job to explore. At the nexus of change is meaning, as conveyed in language: a second given of his position arises from their inseparability.

As Augustine observed, meaning arises from what is signified by the thing, what is signified by the receiver of a message, and the means of communication. Something similar can be said of the way in which the historian reflects reality. At any moment, which is an arbitrary intrusion into a continuously developing set of events, change and perceived or communicated change are not the same. So praxis, the identity of object and subject—which was, it is not surprising, a utopian ideal in the Middle Ages as well as in the nineteenth century when medieval studies were revived—also becomes problematical. Rather, there is *discontinuity*. Social reality, to the degree that it can be encompassed in language, is a compromise between an objectivity that cannot be known *in toto* and a subjectivity that cannot be wholly reflected upon while it is being experienced. It is worth recalling Max Weber's often misunderstood distinction between the pair, which lies at the basis of his conception of meaningful social activity. As he saw it, sociology is to concern itself primarily with the interpretive understanding of society. Action, in this equation, refers to the subjective meaning (*subjektiven Sinn*) the individual attaches to his own behavior, not to some objectively correct or metaphysically true sense.[10] Thus action is "social" insofar as its subjectively organized understanding takes account of the behavior of others and is interrelated with it. Sociology long ago abandoned this priority. Social history cannot afford to do so.

II

If the type of discontinuity I have described is to be seen as an essential ingredient in a sociological outlook, then the properties of literary works cannot be ignored. On the contrary, methods must be developed for dealing with all texts. These methods are an integral part of historical analysis.

Every cultural expression, whether literary, artistic, or musical, is an arbitrary imposition onto reality of a new conjunction of object, subject, and meaning. The historian, as noted, is tempted to treat the literary text, or its equivalent in other domains, as a fact rather than an event, and to reduce its multidimensionality to the flatness of other facts, no matter how they are derived. But, as Durkheim reminds us, a fact is what we think it is. In social history, the object assumed to exist on the outside has only the status of a hypothesis, or, as some would prefer, a myth. As the historian views reality, it is difference, not identity, that is an ineradicable feature of things. Often there is a conflict between the objective and subjective elements he sees. This tension is necessary: at times, it is the essential bond in the social and intellectual whole.

What then of rationality, coherence, and order? They have more to do with professional commitments than with realities. A fully coherent historical picture is a police state: the weapons have merely been concealed. I do not argue, like Foucault, that the only acceptable history is an anti-history. That is going too far. But there must be an examination of internal and external systems of control, in which language and texts play a central role. If the means by which actors interpret reality are ignored, the texts they have made are effectively broken up into a junk heap of facts. History, then, is no longer a disinterested inquiry into rationalities, which is what Max Weber wanted. It becomes an emotionally committed search for Rationality. In a literary no less than in a social sense, this Rationality is a chimaera: the proof is the plasticity of discourse, in which no valid separation can be made between object and subject. The relation between the two is almost always indeterminate—that is, in neither one camp nor the other but shifting between the two.[11]

In this statement I move considerably beyond Weber. Yet there are important connections. Weber's *Idealtypus* is not, as is often proposed, an abstraction based on the common features of a number of so-called objective factors in a social situation. It is a collective idea referring to subjectively construed meanings among actors interpreting a given set of events. As such, it does not view the social system as something divorced from the activity of consciousness. Weber's views, moreover, belong to the mainstream of thinking on the problem of knowledge since Kant. The historian who rejects subjectivity in this sense is similar to the Humean skeptic who disallows all forms of understanding that cannot be registered as isolated sense-impressions of a presumed external world. Kant, of course, argued that objective reality is known only insofar as it conforms to the essential features of the knowing mind. What are known are the things of experience, the phenomena, not the things in themselves, the noumena. Although Weber's vagueness on subjective meaning has been criticized,[12] his synthesis draws together remarkably well the different threads of discussion in Jaspers, Rickert, and Tönnies, thereby providing a bridge between neo-Kantianism and the linguistic aspects of the subject/object problem introduced by Saussure and elaborated in structuralism and poststructuralism. We find a similar line of thinking about consciousness in the thought of Ernst Cassirer.[13] What is common to these positions is the recognition of a problem area *between* subject and object, with conscious thinking as the mediator. The choice for the social and intellectual historian is between participating in a major development in modern thought or adhering to a position that has been abandoned by a substantial number of minds.

The attitudes of historians are not the only problem. There are some serious limitations in recent literary criticism that make its methods difficult to apply to historical materials. One area of concern is relativism, particularly in semiotics. At times, what seems to be suggested is that reality is like a type of symbolism in which it is possible to substitute one thing for another almost at will. This negates the idea of genetic historical development without putting anything really new in its place. Again, the too-rigid opposition of synchrony and diachrony, which is more of a worry in structuralism than in poststructuralism, threatens to erect a new set of barriers between object and subject that even advanced theories of meaning cannot overcome.

I see this as a major issue, and I should like to dwell on it for just a moment. Let us take two idealized positions. The central concern of the student of literature is synchrony. He or she analyses a text as a timeless set of interrelations, through either philology, linguistics, or stylistics. He or she views the text primarily within a literary continuum. The intentions of the author or the work and the relationship to a real or putative audience are also concerns. But the point of departure for the understanding of these interactions is the text itself.

By contrast, the historian is diachronic in perspective. (One can except antihistories, like those of Nietzsche or Foucault, but these presuppose an audience that is already aware of history as a story of continuities.) Whether he or she is empiricist or not, the historian normally wants to place events in a linear sequence. Synchronic elements may be admitted, but they are also assimilated into the continuum of past, present, and future. Categories of analysis are also time-oriented. Rarely in historical writing is the central task envisaged as the analysis of a text on its own. Rather, the dissection of the text is a means to an end. The individuality of the text as an event is minimized, so that the metaphor of sequential patterning can be maintained.

I would argue that, behind much of the theoretical furor in literary studies, these academic attitudes have been left largely unchanged. The devotion to programs is a sort of camouflage, behind which there is no standing army of substantive studies. For historical writing, which can be likened to a science in which the investigator is the experimentor, this is an unsatisfactory situation. It is not possible to historicize literary discussions, nor does it seem likely that historical ones will treat texts as anything but repositories of fact. Conversations take place, but usually from separate tables. If one wants an example of the type of division this sort of dialogue can produce, it is instructive to look at the history of relations between philology and linguistics. Linguistics was born from philology, a historical discipline with a clearly defined diachronic methodology. But within a hundred years it alienated itself from all aspects of history. It is now difficult to introduce historical considerations into linguistic studies, except as anecdotes.

There is nothing new in an adversary relationship between the synchronic and the diachronic. The same issues have appeared with different names throughout Western tradition. The respective positions are first conceptualized by Plato and Aristotle. Plato, although he moved toward a synchronic posture later in life, was known to subsequent philosophers as an intelligent interpreter of the diachronic viewpoint. That is why he was the most popular pagan philosopher in the Latin West during the early Middle Ages. His position, or what was known of it, harmonized easily with the book of Genesis, which saw creation beginning at a definite point in time. To the medievals, this historical development was the primary reality, for which they found strong support in the *Timaeus*. Synchronic elements were later introduced, but between Augustine and Aquinas sequential growth was never seriously questioned. The basic ideas were still alive in the Renaissance, when thinkers finally acquired the full corpus of Plato's works and had at their disposal potent arguments with which to counter such a one-sided view of his mind.

A synchronic view is implicit in Aristotle's criticism of Plato as an unscientific writer. Aristotle was empiricist. He believed that theories should be built up slowly and patiently from a mass of factual details. He presented to later antiquity and the Middle Ages a comprehensive critique of the diachronic view of reality as understood by Plato beginning with the notion that the world and its organizing principles are eternal. In Aristotle, as in his chief medieval commentators, Avicenna, Averroës, and Maimonides, reality is understandable as a system, although a directed one. The search for the laws of nature is separable from the story of how the world became what it is. History is at best a code devised by God so that insufficiently endowed mortals can be presented with complex ideas in a simplified form. In the radical Aristotelian position in the fourteenth century known as Averroism, a number of tenets were specifically put forward against diachrony. It was argued that time had no beginning, the intellect is not unitary, and free will is not a determining force in life. These views, though not those of Aristotle himself, were rejected by the Christian Middle Ages and by Islam, as well as by the majority of Renaissance humanists. But they appeared later. Two influential spokesmen for diachrony, Vico and Marx, both reacted against the synchronic implications of competing philosophies, Vico against Descartes, and Marx against unhistorical political economy.

But the contemporary chapter of the story has a unique quality. This arises from the emphasis on the formal aspects of language and culture, whereas the earlier debates focused on what were thought to be realities. The twentieth-century discussion is the byproduct of a profound moral and philosophical skepticism, and it assumes more radically than does Kantianism that an understanding of external reality is unattainable. Yet that remains the stated goal of much investigation. What is and is not a valid historical explanation is understood better nowadays than ever before. But a price has been paid. This is the abandonment of some areas of inquiry in which forms of behavior and communication intermingle with ideas.

What Marx said about the younger Hegelians, *mutatis mutandis*, can be said about many contemporary theories of the past. The social historian who is interested in ideas has to choose between two unpalatable extremes. One can start off like the ethnographer with fieldwork, piecing together meaningful relations from bits of information, moving, as Victor Turner says, "from experience of social life to conceptualization and intellectual history."[14] But, if one does this, one gives up some pretensions. For individual action is almost never the result of the systematic pursuit of "a grand design."[15] As Mary Douglas puts it, "experience is not amenable" to formal categories.[16]

On the other hand, the historian can begin with the analysis of forms of interpretation. But then one runs the risk of equating historical understanding with the literary form of historical writing. One imprisons the practitioner within the written mode. History becomes an artifact, a work of scholasticism, a museum piece. Doubtless an awareness of this problem has made borderland areas of inquiry like ritual and folklore attractive. There a choice does not have to be made between experience and ideas. But the mainstream of history cannot be nourished by this sort of study alone, and sooner or later the borders must be crossed. Experience must be viewed in the light of typologies, ideas measured against everyday life.[17]

At this juncture the question of meaning is paramount. A distinction must be made between a social history that pretends to be a science of reality, but is chiefly an internalist discipline, and a sociological and anthropological history that allows the question of meaningful interpretation to arise: that is, between a history that permits and one that does not permit a secular ontology. The current debate on language, literature, and form has largely bypassed this issue. All modes of discourse are looked upon from either a conceptual or a rhetorical perspective. The problem of meaning is absorbed into the means of communication, from which it cannot extricate itself without serious loss of credibility. This world is finally one of interchangeable universals.

However, if there is to be a history that engages the problem of meaning, it must first speak as a history. This implies that the movement of forms must end somewhere. I have argued in this essay that the appropriate place is where arbitrary meanings are imposed on presumably impersonal events by those who perceive them. This is admittedly a limited field of interpretation. The meaning may have no relation to the time at which it appears except that it appears at that time. There may be no underlying secret to be wrung, *per allegoriam*, from its Gordian structure, which, as I say, is just the given. This is really all the historian has to work with. His task is not to assemble the evidence like a group of people in a realistic painting, with the result that the conscious design imposes a single, unavoidable interpretation. It is closer to the work of the primitive artist, who molds his symbolic universe anew on each occasion from inherited materials that he cannot change. History, as it is lived, is not rational, not even reasonable; it needs continual decoding, demythologizing, conscious unfolding—in short, the sort of light, of which Spinoza spoke, that not only illuminates the darkness but also itself.

CHAPTER FIVE

LANGUAGE AND CULTURE:
SAUSSURE, RICOEUR, AND FOUCAULT

I

Hannah Arendt began her last set of public lectures with a timely reflection on our everyday sense of reality. Men and animals, she reminded us, "to whom things appear and who as recipients guarantee their reality—are themselves also appearances, meant and able both to see and be seen, hear and be heard, touch and be touched." They are both subjects and objects. "What we usually call 'consciousness,'" she added, "would never suffice to guarantee reality. (Descartes' *Cogito me cogitare ergo sum* is a non sequitur for the simple reason that this *res cogitans* never appears at all unless its *cogitationes* are made manifest in sounding-out or written-down speech, which is already meant for and presupposes auditors and readers as its recipients.)"[1]

What is most interesting in this statement is the parallel between the traditional problem of subject and object, which, in Arendt's thought, goes back to Kant, and the contemporary metaphor of language as a means of describing relationships in reality. The "sounding-out" and "writing-down" to which she refers has become a commonplace for setting forth the manner in which cultural objects are produced, acquire meaning, and play roles in our lives. Such expressions do not strike us as odd. The fact that we take so little notice of them attests to the pervasiveness of metaphors relating the oral and the written in contemporary critical discussion.

Most of these ways of thinking and speaking originated in linguistics or in philosophies of language heavily indebted to linguistic research. A set of technical terms in a discipline with pretensions to scientific rigor was taken over by other fields, notably by literary criticism, intellectual history, and interpretive anthropology, where it merged with, and reinforced, already-existing trends. The appropriateness of the comparisons was not questioned; instead, it became fashionable to introduce them into an increasingly wide orbit of contexts. The rapprochement between linguistic and other descriptive strategies is well established. Language metaphors have even come to rival statistics as a common denominator between history and the social sciences.

One of the purposes of this essay is to question some of the assumptions that underlie such thinking about language, especially the alleged value neutrality of language in the contexts in which the metaphors occur. I begin with a backward look at Saussure, in whom the contemporary tradition of linguistic allegory first takes shape. But the major interest of the essay lies elsewhere: in Ricoeur, in whom an attempt is made to overcome the problems in Saussure at a theoretical level, and in Foucault, who, in my view, is an important contributor to overcoming them in the writing of history. I also offer some suggestions on the ways in which distinctions based upon language, whether spoken or written, may be useful in bridging the gulf between social and literary history, provided that their metaphorical and rhetorical nature is clearly understood.

My point of departure is that the dichotomy between subject and object set up by many language metaphors is more apparent than real. I propose, as does Hilary Putnam, that "the mind and the world jointly make up the mind and the world," adding only that the "world" about which I speak is limited to the historical past; therefore, when I discuss "reference," I am even more emphatically than Putnam thinking of "a relation between a word (or other sort of sign, symbol or representation) and something that actually exists."[2] We have all been taught that words have no necessary connection with their referents; but we should not assume on that account that meaning is just a by-product of our minds or brains.[3] My personal support for this position does not arise from within philosophy, but from the empirical psychology of reading, an admittedly imprecise science, and its potential application to literary and historical issues. At this crossroads, I suggest, some old problems have disappeared and some new ones have come into being.

II

One of the acknowledged father figures for inquiries into language and culture in our time is Saussure. He is not as fashionable as he was a generation ago. It is useful, therefore, to remind ourselves that certain of his ideas represent permanent acquisitions for the theory of culture. I begin with these, which I see as a natural background for developing a somewhat different set of priorities.

If we were to construct a series of elementary parallels between language and culture based upon Saussure, what would they look like?[4] In general, Saussure drew from Durkheim the notion that language, and by implication culture, is at once an entity in itself and a principle of classification. As a consequence, we may speak of both language and culture as having an external side—what is visible, tangible, or heard—and an internal side—what is understood, unarticulated, or unconscious. In Saussure's view, without internality, language and culture are meaningless; without externality, they can neither be perceived nor interpreted.

One is not born with the inner understanding Saussure calls

la langue. Instead, one learns it little by little from infancy to adulthood, and, if we accept a modified Piagetian hypothesis, in definable conceptual stages. Similarly, one's understanding of culture is not an innate genetic code. It is acquired by learning and socialization. Within the heterogeneous group of activities Saussure calls *le langage* one can isolate and study *la langue*; so, within the assembly of activities meaningful to individuals, one can separate and discuss transindividual cultural meaning. One can study the *langue*, but not the *parole*, of a dead language. In the same way one can conduct an archaeological investigation into the historical meaning of any cultural object or activity without knowing the individual circumstances that gave rise to it.

A few further parallels. In Saussure, language use is heterogeneous, while *la langue* is homogeneous. Culture is comparable: while activity meaningful to individuals is heterogeneous, cultural meaning as understood by groups, communities, or societies is homogeneous. Again, *langue* is no less than *parole* a tangible entity (*un objet de nature concrète*). In other words, linguistic signs are perhaps mental in nature, but they are not on that account abstractions. They are cognitive realities. In the same manner one can propose that human activity is not "concrete" while cultural meaning is an abstraction. There is no antithesis between the procedures and their cultural meaning: they are both realities, but of different kinds. Moreover, the signs of a language are tangible in their way, since they are fixed in conventional images by writing. Groups of cultural signs, which I tentatively call "texts," are also given a sensible form through artifacts such as books, buildings, paintings, and so forth. The fixing of language in written form is impossible for *parole*; so too, only meaningful forms of cultural activity, or those purporting to have meaning, can exist as artifacts, as opposed to individual activities to which particular or preexisting meanings are attached. To these ideas we may subjoin Saussure's Aristotelian affirmation that "language is a system of signs expressing ideas." So, for that matter is culture.

Implied in this statement is the idea that language can furnish a model for understanding other systems of signs, and it is here that problems begin for the analogy between language and culture in Saussurean terms. For culture combines various systems of signs into texts, which, as artifacts (that is, as articulated "works" of one kind or another), are no longer reducible to the "languages" out of which they were made. While other systems of signs must acknowledge the primacy of language, culture, as a conglomeration of different sign systems and a unit possessing its own communicative properties, acknowledges language as only one of its components. Paradoxically, then, while languages make up culture, culture is more than the sum of the sign systems that comprise it. Saussure seems to be leading us in this direction when he states that "one can compare *la langue* to a symphony, the reality of which is independent of the manner in which it is executed."[5] By adapting this notion, one can speak of a cultural *langue* as a text and of individual *parole* as an interpretation. And cultural meaning, like *la langue*, can be described as "*un système qui ne connaît son propre ordre.*"[6]

But what about texts? Saussure devotes little space to the problem of speaking versus writing. He sums up his thoughts in chapter six of the Introduction to his *Cours de linguistique générale*, where he refers briefly to *langue* and *écriture*. In his view, the pair are distinct systems of signs, in which the sole raison d'être of writing is to represent what is said. The transcript is foreign to the internal order of language.[7] This position, common to all mainstream structuralist thinking, led inevitably to the problem described by Paul de Man as "the use of grammatical (especially syntactical) structures conjointly with rhetorical structures, without apparent awareness of a possible discrepancy between them."[8] It is axiomatic to contrast

Saussure's approach (which, it is worth noting, does not differ essentially from that of American linguists such as Sapir and Bloomfield) with the early Derrida, in particular with his well-known assertion that writing has its own ontological foundation, which the historical privileging of voice has merely obscured. But this perception has had little influence on the methods of intellectual history. Foucault, for instance, who bestrides structuralism and poststructuralism, chose a middle course. In his inaugural lecture at the Collège de France on December 2, 1970, he returns again and again to the idea of discourse as a verbal phenomenon. Yet, when he explains the power of discourse to limit, to exclude, or to forbid, he is inevitably led to speak of it as a written, codified, and even institutionalized form.[9] His *société de discours* is more than halfway to what I call a "textual community," a group in which there is both a script and a spoken enactment and in which social cohesion and meaning result from the interaction of the two.[10]

One can debate this matter in linguistics or philosophy, but in history there is no purely theoretical solution. At critical moments in the history of culture, societies have oriented themselves around the production of script. They have also assumed that there are close links between rationality and textuality. One does not have to look hard for examples: the transition to the post-Homeric age, the emergence of rabbinic Judaism, the creation of Islam around a single, universalizing text, or the rebirth of literacy in the Middle Ages. At other times the pendulum has swung in the opposite direction. Here, one can refer to the oral communities of pre-Christian Europe or pre-Islamic Asia, to the persistence of oral culture among tribesmen in Africa or Latin America, or to the complex embodying of oral tradition in religions whose adherents claim that their texts are in fact the "word" of God.

Even if one does not accept the determinisms implied in such schematic shifts in taste, and I do not, the fact remains that the linguistic and historical appreciation of writing's role in communication are not the same thing. The written may only be an imperfect copy of the spoken, just as words are perhaps only an approximation of thought. However, within civilizations, writing has always enjoyed a prestige and influence that outweigh its actual functional role. This has come about because a small, but powerful, elite of literati, whether religious, legal, or literary, have always risen successfully to literacy's defense. For better or worse, the course of intellectual history has usually followed their lead. One can put the matter another way by saying that *langue* and *écriture* are not only two distinct systems of signs, but that they are also different in conception and influence. Saussure may have anticipated this notion in his often-quoted statement that "the written word is so intimately intermingled with the spoken word of which it is an image that it finishes by usurping the principal role. One comes to give as much or more importance to the representation of the vocal sign as to the sign itself."[11]

III

One of the recognized problems with all structuralisms is their reductive nature. It is possible to derive from Saussure a picture of language that greatly overemphasizes internal relations. Paul Ricoeur has sought a way out of this impasse. He reminds us that Saussure considered phonology, and by implication any science of discrete linguistic elements, merely as an auxiliary to semantics.[12] The problem with the Saussurean position, as he sees it, arises from the "epistemological weakness of *parole*,"[13] which seems to disappear while the event of *langue* remains. In order to avoid such a radical dichotomy, he suggests that the central event of language lies in discourse.

Ricoeur's thinking on the subject can perhaps be summarized as follows.[14] In his view, the linguistic entity that bears meaning and demands maximum attention is not the word or the sign, as in structuralism, but the sentence. According to Benveniste, in every sentence there are two types of identification at work, the singular, through the subject, and the universal, through the predicate. It is this, rather than the simple opposition of *langue* and *parole*, that establishes the dialectic of event and meaning. If the language system is outside time, discourse is realized within time, and the atemporality of language is revealed to us only in the moment of actualization. Therefore, according to Ricoeur, "if all discourse is actualized as an event, all discourse is understood as meaning."[15]

But what happens when speaking is represented by writing? Ricoeur proposes the well-known disjunction between the message and the medium. Through writing, discourse is fixed, inscribed, and given permanent form in a vehicle external to the human voice, thereby altering the six major factors that Roman Jakobson states are central to all verbal communication (namely, the speaker, hearer, medium, code, situation, and message).[16] For Ricoeur, writing is the chief factor affecting the ambivalence of discourse, which can either disappear like spoken words or be given a changeless form through a text. Moreover, writing transfixes language at the semantic level, since what is preserved is not the event but the said of what is spoken. There is an "intentional exteriorization"[17] of both event and meaning, which now appear as a unit.

When writing replaces speaking, the result is "literature." The face-to-face relations between speaker and hearer are replaced by the relation between writer and reader. The meaning of the speaker and the meaning of the discourse can no longer overlap or be circumscribed by a common subjectivity. Inscription and the semantic autonomy of the text become one, and this results from the disconnection of the author's intention and the text's meaning.[18] The notion of semantic autonomy lies at the basis of all exegesis and hermeneutics. Intentionality is never completely erased, nor is the text ever completely autonomous. However, in a written as opposed to a spoken text, the author is no longer physically present, and the audience, being abstract, is potentially universal. Of course, no literary work is directed toward all of an audience, but rather to a segment of it, a segment that can be defined in economic, social, or cultural terms. In the interplay of text and audience, the work helps to create that very segmented public. Ricoeur adds that the relationship between message and code, which lies at the basis of structuralist analysis, is made much more complicated by the introduction of writing, an elementary fact that most structuralists simply ignore. He also proposes an intelligent modification of the phenomenological approach: for, just as the text frees meaning from the orbit of mental intention, it also liberates the written work from the sphere of situational reference.

These reflections on much discussed themes preface Ricoeur's original use of the idea of discourse to overcome the Gadamerian antinomy of alienation and participation.[19] In Ricoeur's view, the major weakness in Gadamer's approach is his failure to consider texts as privileged mediators between interpretive distance and integrative belonging. "The text," he proposes, "is much more than a particular cause of intersubjective communication: it is the paradigm of distanciation in communication. As such, it displays a fundamental characteristic of the very historicity of human experience, namely that it is communication in and through distance."[20] Distancing need not be viewed, as it was in Romantic hermeneutics, in an entirely negative light; it can also be looked upon as something positive and productive. It is a source of cultural optimism.

We may all agree that "distanciation" lies at the crossroads of history and human experience. But how are we to characterize it? It is here that problems arise. Ricoeur suggests a five-stage process: "(1) the realisation of language as *discourse*; (2) the realisation of discourse as a *structured work*; (3) the relation of *speaking to writing* in discourse and in the works of discourse; (4) the work of discourse as the *projection of a world*; (5) discourse and the work of discourse as the *mediation of self-understanding*."[21]

But is this adequate? It is appropriate as a starting point for an aesthetic and *literary* construction of experience, but it is inadequate as a conceptualization of the aesthetic and *historical* aspects of experience. Worse, it creates a somewhat unnatural barrier between the two. If one were to attempt to integrate historical action into the picture, the scheme would appear more like the following:

1. The realization of language as discourse and its fixation as writing—that is, text production.

2. The use of potential, actual, recalled, and imagined texts to organize experience, structure thought, and guide future activity, along with attendant feedback at each stage.

3. The enactment of texts as living narratives and the organization of life according to their implicit rules, norms, and meanings; through this, the integration of ideas and experience, in which neither has automatic priority.

4. The resulting division of works of discourse into two classes, theory and practice: the one results in a literary work and reflects the triad of discourse, work, and writing[22]; the other refers to the anthropological and historical process by which discourse is transformed into action and in which action is reflected back into discourse. (This process varies from society to society; along with kinship and economic organization, it constitutes one of the fundamental differentiating features of societies.)

All such schemes are crude instruments for dealing with the complexities of actual experience, and the two outlined are deliberately oversimplified. My point in contrasting them, despite their obvious similarities, is to suggest that they are directed toward different ends. Ricoeur's scheme has as its goal a description of hermeneutic experience, and it remains infratextual inasmuch as experience is ultimately reflected through texts. Mine is an attempt to illustrate where texts, seen as adjuncts of discourse, interpenetrate human action (allowing, of course, that action is most often known through texts and that the distinction between thought and action is sometimes arbitrary). My minimal suggestion is that the reality of actual events, however that is conceived, must figure somewhere in the equation of discourse, experience, and the historically describable. I return to my initial position that the mind and the world jointly make up the mind and the world: but there *is* a world.

The issues can be clarified if we push the comparison between Ricoeur's scheme and mine a little further. Ricoeur intelligently separates the problem of writing from that of the text. In a formulation reminiscent of Bakhtin, he states that "it is not writing as such which gives rise to the hermeneutical problem, but the dialectic of speaking and writing."[23] This dialectic is anterior to the opposition of speaking and writing and arises from discourse itself. It is to discourse, therefore, that we must turn "for the roots of all subsequent dialectics."[24] But this way of putting matters runs the risk of relativizing experience and of eliminating historical individuals. Speaking and writing are metaphors for describing thought and experience. It is normal that discourse should exhibit the dual functions of distanciation and participation by means of these means of communication. But the substance of this activity must not be mistaken for the forms through which it is mediated. The dialectic involves reality, not just thoughts about reality: it is influenced by the spoken and written elements in discourse and also by the interplay of language, thought, and action.

Because of the textual bias of his interests, Ricoeur finds it necessary to introduce the "structured work" between the process by which language becomes fixed discourse and the dialectical relations of speaking and writing. "The triad discourse-work-writing . . . only constitutes the tripod which supports the decisive problematic, that of the projection of a world."[25] And this leads eventually to the reconsideration of the classical hermeneutic question of self-understanding. Suppose, however, that we substitute for the structured work the structured act, which has both its worklike and its discourselike sides, and that the link between the two is the communicative bridge we call writing—that is, the fixing of speechlike interaction in a text. Matters are then changed. The triad of discourse, work, and writing may still support a projection of the world, but the triad of action, discourse, and writing is more reflective of the manner in which language interpenetrates life. The world described in these relations is no longer limited by language but becomes the real world, of which language is a part and an expression. (For even if we know reality only through language, we assume that language is not just speaking about itself.) We can now account for the influence of nonrepeatable events upon thought and subsequent experience: the things to which Adam gave names, so to speak, once imprinted or stamped, decisively program our linguistic and conceptual futures.

Saussure contrasted the linguistic event, which is a temporal phenomenon, with the system of language, which is outside time. In transforming his distinctions, hermeneutics prefers to speak of discourse as the event of language, referring back not only to the speaker, as Benveniste suggests, or to the implied dialogue between speaker and hearer, but rather "to a world which it claims to describe, express or represent"; Ricoeur argues that the event in this sense "is the advent of a world in language by means of discourse."[26] But here again, language is really talking about itself rather than the real world. When a historian speaks of an event, however obscure the notion may actually be, he means principally something that happens once and only once. Discourse cannot be a model for this sort of happening because discourse ultimately refers back to an inner code or meaning rather than to an outer succession of activities over time, while the historical event is unique in gaining its meaning both from a logic within the mind of man and in the outside world as well. In this sense Christ's crucifixion was an unprecedented *event*.

Furthermore, the external nature of an event may set in motion a pattern of thought and action that shapes future configurations. The gospel narratives, which are detached in time from the real life of Christ, but inseparable from Christian life thereafter, are an example. Here, to allude to an old controversy, it can be asked whether the eternal chain of events that constitutes historical change does not have more in common with the physical sciences than with hermeneutic understanding, which often acts like an afterthought or a transcript of actual experience. The succession of events in reality exhibits none of the rationality of a textual world homologous with *langue* and *parole*, which acquires meaning because *la langue* is coherent. The chain of events is essentially irrational by these criteria, as medieval allegorists maintained in the conviction that one could almost always understand reality through language. Yet this is not the case. If one were to compare the succession of physical events in history to an aspect of linguistic experience as outlined by Saussure, perhaps the most sensible place to locate it would be in the original imposition of signs. And this, Saussure wisely states, like the problem of the origin of language, is not properly speaking a subject of linguistic research at all.

However, there is one aspect of hermeneutic analysis that is directly relevant to this discussion. Earlier I referred to Ricoeur's statement to the effect that while all discourse is understood as meaning, all discourse is realized as event. For hermeneutics, what counts is the preserved meaning, not "the fleeting event." But the historian is equally interested in the structures of meaning that may have informed the real event (in older terminology, its intellectual background) of which the actual event may represent an articulation or exteriorization, rather in the way that revolutions are prepared in advance by a series of scarcely visible changes in economy and society. One can agree with Ricoeur that articulation is at the heart of the problem: "Just as language, by being actualised in discourse, surpasses itself as system and realises itself as event, so too discourse, by entering the process of understanding, surpasses itself as event and becomes meaning."[27] By the same token, history, by becoming a text, surpasses itself as a set of real events and is realized as a structure of meaning, thereby acquiring the capacity to be interpreted. And, just as the individual discourse attests to the speaker's intended meaning, so history, as a combination of articulated events and patterns of understanding, bears witness to a broader type of intentionality, such as may be found in the group, the community, or the nation. Here again, events are "surpassed by meaning."

Let us take this line of thinking one stage further. The final result of the hermeneutic process is the metamorphosis of the discourse into the work, while the final result of the social organization of written knowledge is the formation of textual communities. According to Ricoeur, a literary work has three characteristics: it is longer than a sentence, and therefore raises new problems of understanding; it reflects a type of codification that is revealed by style, genre, and other literary qualities; and its configuration is unique, as no two works are alike.[28] A text that informs a group, gives a context to intersubjective thoughts, and leads to action is likewise ordered in the same way. Taking the three conditions in reverse order: since the actual events that constitute history are unique, each record or account is a literary individual. Such works, and the event-structures on which they are based, exhibit all the qualities we would expect to find in the narrative genre known as history. And, like the other works, they are not merely semantic units constructed out of unrelated sentences. They are semantic maps for the exploration of new territory.

But there are differences as well. I referred above to the potential division of discourse into literary works, in the normal sense, and the type of discourse that enters and exits from the historical process itself. Ricoeur's typology accounts for the production of cognitive structures, whether they are based on reality or on fiction. It does not tell us all that we would like to know about the interpenetration of written structures with reality. In this case, the logic of event and meaning operates in a different way. Meaning comes first. A text, proposed by one member of a group, is understood by the others in a similar way, like certain statements in the gospels about the spiritual life that might lead one to think that marriage was a bad thing. In this instance, one text has given rise to another, the second being a combination of the original and an interpretation. It is the second that influences behavior: the members of the group, having imbibed the message, go forth into the world – not the world of language, or of speech acts, but the world of events – and carry out actions based upon their textually informed beliefs, like divorcing their wives. These beliefs have acquired the force of moral imperatives.

Alienation also operates differently. In hermeneutics the sole medium of self-understanding is the text, which is subjectively appropriated by the reader.[29] But when texts inform patterns of life and vice versa, as happens, for instance, in the medieval pilgrimage, the field of interpretive possibilities is considerably enlarged. There may be similarities between the narratives of texts and the narratives of life. But appropriation, as Marx stresses, involves the real world: it is an overcoming, not only of the problems introduced by writing and objectification, but of the conflicts of reality. We understand ourselves, Ricoeur correctly notes, "by the long detour of the signs of humanity deposited in cultural works."[30] Yet there are still longer detours: for example, the manner in which our preexisting values, sense of meaning, and education are shaped by experience, or the manner in which memory, reminiscence, and the unconscious play out roles in our everyday lives, compelling us, as Freud stresses, to enact dramas whose ultimate meaning may be hidden from us.

IV

At this point it is appropriate to turn briefly to Foucault. I have referred above to his unusual ability to capitalize on both the verbal and textual components of discourse and thereby to bridge the structuralist and poststructuralist *mentalités*. He did this in part through a remarkable style, which managed to be rhetorical and analytical at once (and which for this reason translates rather poorly into English, in which the two functions are normally separate).

Foucault also left a permanent legacy in the history of relations between ideas and society. The positive side of the legacy arises from the recognition that, in societies, the production of discourse is controlled, selected, organized, and redistributed by a number of procedures. These operate from within the mind and tell us automatically what is permitted or forbidden, what is rational or insane, and what is true or false.[31] But there is a negative side, which results from too great a concern with two elements in the process, production and power. A tendency to overemphasize these factors grew progressively through the respective studies of madness, Enlightenment thought, and sexuality; and over concern with a small, if admittedly important, set of issues inevitably left many other questions unanswered. One of these was the precise manner in which one proceeds from thought to action in a variety of historical situations. Another was the relation of the individual to the group. To the end, Foucault never really came to grips with authorship or intentionality as they operate through texts in history. Overall, and especially in his last works, one senses a lack of equilibrium. The thesis is a little too strong: by avoiding all overt structures of interpretation, Foucault invariably imposes his own interpretive voice on everything. One mode of explanation, his personal discourse, acquires by the default of others the illegitimate capacity to universalize.

Foucault's best books—one thinks of *Les mots et les choses*—are masterpieces of a genre. It is a genre of irony, skepticism, and disenchantment, not a vision of an age that was, but as with Theodor Adorno, a rebellion against the idea that the "ages" of standard history could ever have existed. The studies are inimitable: Foucault had no students, wanted no disciples. We are still attempting to sort out the type of narrative he wrote.[32] In one respect, however, Foucault is part of the discussion I have traced through Saussure and Ricoeur. His plea on behalf of the hidden plasticity of discourse occasionally sounds like an echo from another age: from antiquity perhaps, when the supremacy of the verbal arts was established; or more aptly, from the later Middle Ages, when it was first successfully challenged by the rise of literacy and textuality; or, if the notion is not too far-fetched, from the moment when ahistorical sociology was born from empirical historical research, since his idea of *discours*, at least in its productive side, reminds one of the nostalgia for *Gemeinschaft*, the small community of speakers, hearers, and face-to-face relationships obscured and obliterated by the internalization of texts, methods, orders, disciplines, and prejudices. In this sense, there is an expression of hope in Foucault's inner concerns that is belied, perhaps deliberately, by his rebellious style.

He also takes us to the doorstep of a problem that is central in intellectual history. Somewhere on the infinitely varied spectrum linking words, semantic units, and finally privileged works, stands a range of texts and their primitive communities of understanding, bracketed, to use Husserl's term, at some middle stage between experience and thought, loosely enough structured to admit variations from real life and yet sufficiently patterned to give some shape to otherwise formless events. It is possible to look for such texts, as Foucault did, in the minor works of a period, as they would appear to preserve a flexibility lacking in the great books. However, it is arguable that their principles are better illustrated in forms of life themselves, whether these are organized as texts or productive of them; whether they discover, or rediscover, the inner rules of conduct, kinship, and thought, which they exteriorize, or whether they acknowledge exterior boundaries that they interiorize, forget, and selectively remember. In my view it is an error to focus on the written text alone. The essential element is the community, the living people whose minds are peopled and shared by thoughts, intentions, and potential actions. The normal hermeneutic activity is the experience of the text along with individual interpretations. In the textual community, as I see it, there is a similar process at work, but here the interpretive variants are derived from thought and life, the forms of life having the same spontaneity as verbal glosses on a written text. Each community creates its culture, subjectively perceiving and objectively constructing new texts. These texts are new worlds, which, once invented, can then be represented, recreating eternal patterns of thought and action anew.

CHAPTER SIX

MAX WEBER, WESTERN RATIONALITY,
AND THE MIDDLE AGES

A name that has appeared frequently in the preceding pages is that of Max Weber. A historian interested in ideas and society is virtually bound to find convenient points of reference in Weber's writings. Beyond that, I suggest that his concept of the subjective element in meaningful social relations is essential for understanding how a textual community works. But there is an important difference between Weber's approach to social relations and what has been presented in this volume. Weber said little about orality and literacy. He did not speculate at length on how a society's means of communication shapes attitudes toward thinking or behavior.

In this essay I look at the absence of this aspect of cognitive development in his work from two perspectives. In the first part, I use medieval science and technology as a point of departure for analysing three weaknesses in his sociology resulting from neglect or misunderstanding of the Middle Ages. My question is what this gap in his otherwise impressive historical learning meant for his outlook as a whole. But this is only the preface to another sort of inquiry. In the second part, I turn to the broader changes brought about by the rise of literacy in the Middle Ages, especially as they affected the values and norms of behavior. The historical evidence, I conclude, compels us to reformulate the development of rationalization as Weber envisaged it.

I

During the past fifty years, progress has been made in our understanding of every aspect of medieval science and technology. Yet we have no commonly accepted model for interpreting these changes within the overall environment of society and culture. What we have is bits and pieces of different models. These are tied together by a number of assumptions that are all too rarely analysed in depth.

If we are to find a way out of this specialist labyrinth, we must address two issues at once. One concerns inherited interpretations, which, with Thomas Kuhn, we may call the normal science of medieval science. The other involves the broader social and intellectual context of premodern history. The central question is this: why did medieval science and technology develop in a manner uncharacteristic of the ancient world, or, for that matter of any previously known society?

By framing the issues in this way, I do not mean to suggest that there have been no attempts to come to grips with larger questions. But the inability to match the particular and the general to which I refer has been voiced by a number of scholars, most notably by the late Lynn White, Jr.[1] The lack of general hypotheses is all the more noticeable in view of the important advances on specialist topics that have been made since the publication of Charles Homer Haskins' *Studies in the History of Mediaeval Science* in 1924. A collective history that appeared in 1979 highlighted some of the principal areas of inquiry in the intervening years.[2] These include the textual transmission of Greek and Arab learning to the West, the institutional and philosophical context of Aristotelian natural philosophy, and the interdependence of ideas in key fields of innovation, such as statics, dynamics, mathematics, optics, and astronomy. Other areas of interest have been explored: the role of the universities in providing a home for scientific thinking,[3] for instance, and the dependence of mathematical skills on commercial developments, especially in Italy.[4]

The occasional surfacing of larger issues in such studies is not to be ignored. Yet their influence on general models of interpretation has been slight. As soon as one turns from devices and disciplines to broader questions, the historiographical picture begins to blur. By and large, the field is still viewed as a set of isolated stories of success or failure, with both the benefits and the limitations imposed by a linear, internalist, and evolutionary perspective. If our understanding is to move to a higher level, we cannot be satisfied with merely occasional statements of general trends. We must return to our point of departure in the inquiry and think our presuppositions through again.

Those who work in the field of medieval science trace the beginnings of professional activity to such influential figures as Pierre Duhem, Georges Sarton, and Lynn Thorndike. Students of the history of technology have fewer dominant voices in their past, partly because of the fragmented nature of technical invention and partly because researchers have less persistently sought the type of respectability that, rightly or wrongly, is conferred on those associated with theoretical science. But internalist histories of technology have also appeared, either aligning themselves with standard narratives in science or with economic and social change.

These studies provide a foundation for further explorations into little-known regions. However, if we wish to examine the cultural roots of the early modern scientific outlook, in which medieval strengths and weaknesses are implicated, we must acknowledge that the beginnings of serious reflection lie in a completely different domain. It was Max Weber who first focused attention on the potential links between science, technology, rational action, and economic or social circumstances. Medievalists are no less heirs to the Weberian tradition than are the historians of later times to whom he more specifically directed his works. If we are to straighten out our thinking about the cultural background of science and technology, we must first revise our thinking about Max Weber and the Middle Ages.

It is customary to divide the evolution of Weber's ideas into three phases. In 1904 and 1905 he published his well-known essay *Die protestantische Ethik and der Geist des Kapitalismus*. He spent the following five years or so defending his thesis on the connections between Calvinism and the rise of Western capitalism. Between 1911 and 1913 a second phase of activity was begun, during which time Weber compiled the section on the sociology of religion in *Wirtschaft und Gesellschaft*, incorporating the important distinction between asceticism and mysticism from his reply to Ernst Troeltsch at the first meeting of the Deutsche Gesellschaft für Soziologie in Frankfurt in 1910.[5] The third phase consisted of a set of revisions of earlier material, which appeared as articles in the *Archiv für Sozialwissenschaft und Socialpolitik* between 1914 and 1917 and were later collected, along with a somewhat revised version of *The Protestant Ethic*, in the three-volume *Gesammelte Aufsätze zur Religionssoziologie*, the first fascicule of which Weber was editing shortly before his death in 1920.[6]

Early students of Weber, particularly in the English-speaking world, directed their attention chiefly to *The Protestant Ethic*, which has been discussed at length at both a historical and sociological level.[7] But the emphasis on one issue inevitably left others in neglect. Little interest was shown in Weber's evangelical family background, which helped to shape his outlook.[8] Nor was there a widespread awareness of how his ideas on power, authority, and legitimation grew naturally out of his perception of the German political situation before World War I.[9] The focusing on a single work within a large, unfinished, and somewhat disorganized corpus also created the impression of inflexibility. Weber was isolated artificially from Marx and Nietzsche, with whom he shared many concerns, as well as from his friends like Tönnies, Simmel, and Troeltsch, with whom he often debated.

Only with the appearance of a mature intellectual biography, and the promise of a critical edition of his works, has there emerged a better understanding of the chronological growth of his mind and the full range of his interests. The shift in emphasis has significantly changed our interpretation of his sociology of religion. The comparative as opposed to purely evolutionary aspect of his investigations has been made clear. In this respect, research has been diverted from *The Protestant Ethic*, and to a lesser extent from the methodological introduction to *Economy and Society*, to the final statement of his views in *The Economic Ethics of World Religions*. Above all, the earlier focus on theory and methodology to the neglect of historical considerations has been replaced by a more balanced view, which sees one of the recurring issues in his work as the process of rationalization in Western society.[10] Rationality, in this sense, is not analysed in isolation as the promoter of one economic outlook, but is looked upon, as Weber intended, "within the totality of cultural development."[11]

These research trends have emerged within German scholarship on Weber since World War II. They permit us to distinguish between Weber's own thoughts and the mass of interpretive material that inevitably springs up around a seminal thinker. They also allow us to isolate certain imperfections in Weber's historical and methodological constructs, the blame for which can no longer be laid on the doorstep of his North American enthusiasts. Three of these are of particular importance for a reassessment of evidence from the Middle Ages.

One is his inadequate education in medieval philosophy and theology. Even those who oppose his interpretation of Reformation thought acknowledge that he made useful distinctions among the theological views of the Lutherans, Calvinists, Pietists, Methodists, and Baptists. Yet he was in the habit of lumping all pre-Reformation theology together into a single, overgeneralized world-picture, which he referred to as "Catholic thought." Within that picture, the only thinker who received more than cursory attention was Thomas Aquinas. The diversity of patristic and early medieval views was not discussed, nor did Weber distinguish between later medieval tendencies based upon Aristotelian or Augustinian foundations.

Weber also made a number of questionable assumptions about other aspects of medieval cultural life. He took the affirmations of the papacy, church councils, and official thinkers as the norm for practices. He did not consider pastoral activity, local hagiographical traditions, or the stimulation offered to the medieval church through heresy and dissent. As a consequence, he assumed a closer harmony between institutions and ideas than existed in reality.

Worse, he focused his historical interests on too narrow a time frame for the adequate observation of long-term changes. Like Marx, with whom in this respect he had much in common, he saw a single, great period of rapid change at the end of the Middle Ages, with the breakup of feudalism and the emergence of urban society. He paid little attention to the centuries that intervened between the Carolingian dynasty and the fourteenth century, an epoch that was under serious reassessment even when he was writing.

Weber's view of medieval mentalities, then, was somewhat schematic. He recognized the differences between medieval and early modern religious thought, and in particular between the scholastic method and the more open, worldly, and scientifically oriented way of looking at things after the Reformation. But there was a basic flaw in his thinking about the two ages: he saw the one as being entirely constrained by institutional boundaries, while the other allowed its great minds to operate outside them. In reality, there was more conformity in Reformation thought than Weber saw, and more productive variety in the Middle Ages than he was willing to grant.

The second major weakness in the medieval aspects of Weber's sociology of religion arises from the much-discussed relationship between tradition and modernity.[12] Weber's model of rationalization brilliantly analysed the advent and progress of modernity. Rationalization in this sense was virtually the same as modernization. But he failed to account adequately for the continuity and evolution of tradition, or for that matter to present a clear definition of what he meant by tradition. In Weber, Edward Shils notes, "the persistence of past practices and arrangements is not taken up as something to be explained."[13] And what is not explained is assumed not to have changed.

If we transfer this way of thinking to the historical dimension of Weber's work, it means, broadly speaking, that the Middle Ages are identified with tradition and the Reformation with modernity. The Middle Ages are static, the postmedieval period dynamic. Three generations of research have produced a more nuanced picture, in which "the revolt of the medievalists," as Wallace Ferguson terms it,[14] has corrected the distortions of early scholarship in the Renaissance and the Reformation. Yet this work has had more influence on articles, monographs, and specialized studies than on general historiography. A version of the early modern hypothesis—which effectively compresses change into a brief, transitional period between the Middle Ages and the Renaissance—still presides over much investigation into the borderland area between science, other types of causality, and society. No better example of this approach can be cited than Keith Thomas's *Religion and the Decline of Magic*, in which the remarkable discussions of astrology, prophecy, witchcraft, and other occult beliefs are all played out against the backdrop of what is called "the magic of the medieval church."[15]

Once again I must make my position clear. I am not arguing that there is no transition from "tradition" to "modernity," however we term it. Nor is historical understanding much advanced if we try, as have some medievalists, to push the Reformation back into the Middle Ages. Yet, by applying the tradition/modernity dichotomy to areas of life and thought in which it does not belong, we inevitably finish in a position of ideological polarization. By the way in which we pose the problem of change, we rule out asking important questions; and, as a consequence, we oversimplify historical development generally. As it turns out, since Weber made his woeful prediction about the imminent extinction of tradition, modernization has not proven to be the irresistible force he envisaged; and, if one looks at the cases of Japan, Israel, or Saudi Arabia, tradition and radical innovation have not always been incompatible.

In medieval history, too, the further back one goes, the more varied are the roles of the forces we facilely group under the heading of tradition. If one wishes to gain a valid overview of how science and technology interpenetrated medieval society between the eleventh and the fourteenth centuries, one must begin by broadening the notion of tradition at least far enough for it to become a workable analytical tool. For if medieval society did not change through a link between rationality and modernization, as did preindustrial England or Germany, it must have changed through unexplored links between rationality and tradition. As curious as it may seem to a generation of historians reared on the notion of unidirectional progress, medieval rationality and rationalization, to use Weber's vocabulary, were by-products of the intensification of the search for traditions.

The third imperfection of Weber's sociology of religion as it applies to medieval research is a methodology that for its time and place is one of its chief strengths: the employment of ideal types. By their use, cultural change is viewed as acting in close harmony with economic and social transformations, if it is not determined by them. Studies attempting to explain relations between culture, society, and economy have long operated under the assumptions of a tripartite construction of reality in which the consideration of religion or the intellectual life is subordinated to material change and social organization. This model—if one may comfortably speak of it in the past tense—had the virtue of reflecting the Marxist concern with superstructure as well as a type of functionalism in which, Clifford Geertz notes, the rituals, symbols, and ideas interdependent with behavior were taken to be supportive of the social materials out of which they were constructed.

The historical counterpart of this position leads us once again to the worst features of the early modern hypothesis. Presented in a general form, the argument is that because we associate the scientific revolution with the sixteenth and seventeenth centuries, we must seek from within that time frame the other components of the modernization process, relegating to the Middle Ages, as to all other earlier periods, mere anticipations of modernity. As a consequence of this textbook version of the past, many contemporary interpretations of the modernization process are emphatically post-medieval in orientation. One unfortunate by-product is to legitimize ignorance of the past—why study remote ages of history, after all, if they are marginal to what one wants to explain? The final result of this sort of thinking is an educated anti-intellectualism, in which medievalists have played an indirect role. For, to the degree that they envisage their task as a mere pushing back of the boundary of modernity, they become unwitting accomplices of those who wish to assign their period of study to a realm of historical unimportance.

Another approach is possible. What men and women regard as life's physical or social necessities is often shaped by elements that are not visible at a given moment in the environment. The causes of change may originate in the lifetime of the individuals who actually experience the changes in question. But, most often, they are prepared well ahead. Weber himself knew this: when he looked at subjectivity, he took account of an individual's past as well as his or her present. If we direct this type of analysis to the problem of medieval science and technology, it is clear that too much attention has been focused on a narrow band of time. We have only begun to understand the role played by cultural and religious forces between the end of the ancient world and the fourteenth century.

In sum, we cannot turn for answers on the large issues to any of the standard formulas of the past—the internalist histories, the unmodified Weberian sociology of religion, the mere pushing back in time of what we call modernity, or the reduction of cultural change to some combination of economic and social forces. The social relations of science and technology are not understood because we do not understand the problem of tradition and modernity by which they are circumscribed.

II

If we wish to advance the question further, we must look at the issues in a different perspective.

At the center of Weber's synthesis we find certain assumptions about rationality and rationalization processes. In my view, this is where the major difficulty lies. What is needed is a revision in the way we tackle this problem.

It may be helpful if I begin with a brief statement of my own thoughts. I believe that the Middle Ages are a more important period in the history of rationality than has previously been acknowledged. This reevaluation is based on consideration of a factor Weber and other classical sociologists overlooked: the rebirth of a literate society in western Europe after the eleventh century, and the concomitant appearance, or reappearance, of a number of important links between literacy and rationality.

This transformation involved the four types of rationality we associate with Weber, the instrumental, substantive, practical, and theoretical.[16] But it was not a specific type of rationality that literacy favored: it provided a tool for the analysis of all that was considered rational, offered a vocabulary, as well as methods based on reading, writing, and pragmatic discourse, through which the objective and subjective aspects of experience could be isolated and conveniently discussed.

The changes in attitudes, perceptions, and thinking that literacy brought about are best observed in religion, the dimension of culture most accessible to the majority of people. Medieval religious life is also the source of another of Weber's favorite themes, the notion that modernity is a mixed blessing. The rise of literacy sheds light on both sides of the question. Reading and writing fostered some economically productive rationalization at an institutional level, but they also accelerated the debate within medieval culture on the limits of reason. With the advent of literacy—that is, of individual readers and writers—that debate entered the mainstream of early modern thought. The discussion contributed to the transforming of an abstract conception of rationality into the positions for and against reason that are the beginnings of preindustrial polemics over tradition and modernity.

Weber wrote no work specifically devoted to medieval religion, although there is evidence that he intended to do so. The hiatus has been a source of distress to his admirers, and various reasons have been advanced to explain the embarrassing silence in an otherwise wide-ranging set of studies in comparative religion. I have already mentioned Weber's oversimplification of medieval thought. But stronger reasons for the lacuna may perhaps be found in his repeated bouts of ill health and in his reluctance to enter the privileged terrain of his colleague and friend Ernst Troeltsch, on whose views about medieval intellectual development he increasingly relied after 1907. Wolfgang Schluchter also suggests that there is a basic weakness in Weber's method in the history of ideas.

Levels and units of analysis are changed frequently and without explanation," which inevitably gives his work a "fragmentary character."[17]

There have also been problems in sorting out just what Weber meant by rationality, and in charting how his views changed over time. Thanks to Reinhard Bendix, Günther Roth, Schluchter, and the specialized inquiries of Stephen Kalberg and Donald Levine, we are in a better position than ever before to come to grips with Weber's notion.[18] It is now agreed that there are two interrelated issues: rationality in general, as it manifests itself in different times, places, and cultures; and "Western rationality," as Weber understood it, which is linked to decisive transformations in Europe during the Reformation.[19] As S. N. Eisenstadt notes, Weber never fully explored the comparative dimension of the subject.[20] His point of repair was always Protestantism and capitalism. Similarly, Weber never really considered alternative historical hypotheses. As his thesis was inextricably linked to actual historical changes, what are we to do if it turns out that he did not understand them adequately?

In contradistinction to what Weber proposed, the historical evidence suggests that the Middle Ages were the period in which rationality began to play a significant role in Western society and culture. The fundamental transformation was made possible by a "carrier" he does not discuss at length, the change from oral to written communications.

Weber appears to have been sensitive to this problem when he discussed other cultures. For instance, in his study of ancient China, he emphasized the role played by literati. He even went so far as to suggest that the ideographic type of writing, in retaining "its pictorial character, was not rationalized into an alphabetical form."[21] By contrast, in Weber's many analyses of Western rationalization processes, we find no significant degree of interest in relations between the means of communication and social or economic organization. But it is in this area that a new understanding has emerged of the part played by later ancient and medieval culture in the history of rationality.

As far as the medieval outlook is concerned, the initial phase of change took place between A.D. 200 and 600 and consisted of three elements. One was the emergence of a new cursive writing, which was in use everywhere but the imperial Roman chancery by the middle of the third century. This greatly enhanced writing's ability to convey the phonetics, grammar, and syntax of what was actually said. An even more important development occurred in book production. The papyrus roll was gradually replaced by the parchment or vellum codex, the forerunner of the modern book. The triumph of the codex was complete by the late third or early fourth century, and was made possible, it is thought, by a long-established tradition of Christians living in Rome, who were in the habit of copying the Bible into parchment notebooks. The codex was more durable than the roll, and easier to read and to store; it facilitated indexing, searching for facts, and the accumulation of reference knowledge characteristic of the much later age of print. But it owed its success less to technical than to political factors: the Bible, as transmitted by codices, became the official sacred book of ancient society after the imperial recognition of Christianity by Constantine I in A.D. 313. In addition to writing habits and book formats, there was an even more basic change in communications during this period. This was the appearance of a linguistic community in western Europe that was the forerunner of the present-day speakers of the Romance languages. The transformation began with the division of Latin into learned and popular forms. Much later, these became identified with written Latin and spoken Romance traditions.

Each century of the Middle Ages has a chapter to contribute to the story of literacy's decline, rebirth, and development in the medieval West. But, with respect to rationality, there is one period of particular importance. It begins in the Carolingian empire of the ninth century, and, despite occasional setbacks brought about by invasions and internal disorder, it reorients an entire set of institutions by the beginning of the thirteenth. A convenient vantage point from which to view the changes in society and culture is found in the history of law. On the Continent, the literate legal revival established three rational fields of jurisprudence, Roman law, canon law, and the codification of statutes. Beginning in Anglo-Saxon times, a parallel evolution in England led to the sealed writ and the beginnings of royal courts. From the latter sprang other literate deputations, such as the exchequer, the bench of common pleas, and the system of itinerant justices. During the twelfth century in both Roman and common law, written documents replaced oral testimony unsupported by evidence, and objective methods for evaluating claims superseded duels, ordeals, and compurgations. The new method consisted essentially of listening to witnesses, analysing the factors in a case, and scrutinizing the written records. This legal renaissance went hand in hand with a growth in expertise in diplomatics, in textual criticism, and in the authentication of acts. People began to think of facts not as recorded by texts but as embodied in texts, a change in mentality of major importance in the rise of methods for classifying, encoding, and retrieving written information. The search for facts, hitherto limited to memory, now shifted to the written page. The great codifications of the twelfth century—Peter Lombard's *Sentences*, Abelard's *Sic et Non*, and Gratian's *Decretum*—were inseparable from a different attitude toward the organization of knowledge. At a more mundane level, the same period saw the rise of types of written records for administering society in northwestern Europe. Some records were kept by individuals, such as charters, testimonials, wills, and sealed memoranda. Other records were compiled by institutions as a permanent reminder of past practices and as a set of guidelines for the future. These included surveys, court rolls, yearbooks, cartularies (or registers), and chronicles.

Many new forms of record-keeping had economic purposes. They went hand in hand with the growth of markets, towns, and a prolonged commerical revolution. Between the eleventh and the thirteenth centuries, the links that Weber saw between rationality and economic activity also made their first appearance. Population increased, and formerly isolated communities came into everyday contact with each other. Entrepreneurial lords sponsored local markets. Cash crops and surpluses emerged as peasants began to introduce crop rotation, metal implements, deeper plowing, and new high-protein foods, rich in energy. All of this in turn contributed to the rise of a money economy, and coinage began to circulate for the first time since the decline of the Roman imperial administration. The commercial revolution was centered in the Italian city-states: by 1100, the wealth of Genoa, Pisa, and Venice had surpassed that of the richest business communities of the ancient world. In the north, the most active markets took place at the fairs of Champagne and Brie. But it was Italian merchants who created the demand for northern textiles, on which the fairs depended, and it was Italian financial arrangements that permitted long-distance transactions to take place in an atmosphere of confidence and mutual trust. The replacement of barter by currency, the emergence of banking and credit, and, by the fourteenth century, the introduction of double-entry accounting were symptomatic of a new mentality. One only has to glance at the materialistic concerns of Chaucer's pilgrims or the monetary metaphors of Nicole d' Oresme to sense the pressures of an economically driven process of rationalization.

III

By these examples we are brought back to the subject of Weber's 1889 doctoral dissertation, *Zur Geschichte des Handelsgesellschaften im Mittelalter.* But there we do not find the issues discussed. There is no place in Weber's reflections on medieval business organization, or in his later works on religion and economic change, for links between rationality and modes of communication.

The appearance of this problem orientation, as well as much of the ancient and medieval evidence to deal with it, belongs to intellectual developments since Weber's day. Three disciplines in particular have added important elements to the theoretical picture. One is philosophy, in which rationality is seen to be inseparable from issues in language. Another is psychology, which views rationality as a topic in cognitive development. Still another is anthropology, which has taught us that there are many non-Western types of rationality. I mention these well-known areas of achievement as a reminder of a perspective that must be maintained in dealing with a thinker from an earlier epoch. We cannot pretend that time has stood still and apply Weber's ideas to the Middle Ages as one might have done in his time. Nor is it flattering to the living tradition of his thought to analyze his basic concepts in an intellectual vacuum.

The changes in our way of approaching rationality to which I refer all point to an accommodation between the rational, conceived as an object of thought, and the means of expression in individuals or society. An important contemporary who realizes this is Jürgen Habermas, in whose *Reason and the Rationalization of Society* the criterion of rationality is the set of claims ordinary speech actors make in establishing the validity of their statements in dialogues, arguments, or other types of interchange.[22] Habermas offers many insights that cannot be related in detail here. He also takes seriously Weber's account of historical rationalization, which he recapitulates.

But Habermas's work has a weakness that is shared by other purely theoretical discussions in this area. He assumes the presence of a literate community of speakers and hearers, for whom the logical and dialogical operations he describes as rational are normal.

They take place within a consensus about what rationality is, and this consensus is supported by the literate institutions of society. How do we deploy this model when these assumptions do not hold? Do they permit us to analyze communications in archaic societies, where the reference system for language is different from that of literate communites?

Clearly we face a dilemma. For a theory of discourse that depends for its criteria of validity on the spoken speech patterns of living actors is ill equipped to deal with societies whose conventions of speech behavior exhibit what Walter Ong calls primary orality. This problem is complicated by two others: the orality in question is known only through texts; and, as we review the evidence from a modernist standpoint, we inevitably incorporate into our thinking the cumulative experience of our own society, in which there is a well-documented passage from the oral to the written.

These issues limit the inquiry from the outset, and there is no final answer to the questions they raise. But their very recognition may act as a warning against relying too much either on a theory that grows out of the medieval evidence or upon one that is a by-product of contemporary thinking. The best we can do is to try to achieve a balance between the demands of each. This means reorienting the large arsenal of today's theory toward the reconstruction of oral and written traditions within the context of evolving social organization. We want to know about the connections between literacy and rationality. But we also want to know how these connections have affected our overall understanding of rationality.

One result of this sort of inquiry is to reduce our tendency to regard rationality as monolithic and to make us take note of pluralism. For the Middle Ages, like any age, saw the rise of different types of rational discourse at the same time. These expressions of rationality were not always in touch with each other. Nor was there a straightforward evolution. Oral and written forms merely answered the needs of different systems of causality. The individual who accepted the notion of abstract justice implicit in Roman law could also pray at the site of a local shrine for a direct intervention to cure illness, relieve poverty, or guarantee salvation. If there is a dominant method in the premodern evidence, I suggest it lies somewhere between theory and practice on the ill-defined border that Weber drew between the value-rational (*wertrational*) and the instrumentally rational (*zweckrational*). On the one hand, there is the "conscious belief in the value for its own sake of some ethical, aesthetic, religious or other form of behavior," which, in the Middle Ages, increasingly became identified with literate systems. On the other, there is a group of "expectations . . . conditions or means for the attainment of the actor's own rationally pursued and calculated ends."[23] As society became more aware of literate norms, these merged with audience relations in a world of speaker and reader response.

How did such changes take place? As illustrations, I offer three medieval cultural developments in which the rise of a more literate society played a role: (1) the rise of dissent and the critical (or scientific) intelligence; (2) the growth of interest in subjectivity, individuality, and the interior life; and (3) the appearance of early forms of the modernist debate on rationality in one area of medieval theology, penance.

I begin with the best known of the three. The awakening of the critical spirit in the Middle Ages has long been the subject of historical research designed to counter the image of a changeless and authoritarian medieval Church. Polemics aside, it is clear that criticism is equally alive among dissenters and reformers. The early reformers, who date from the ninth century, all championed literate standards in liturgy, monastic life, and ecclesiastical organization. Later advocates of reform emphasized similar principles, whether they were wandering preachers, Gregorian propagandists, or leaders of new religious orders. The impulse toward textual organization in medieval religious movements reached its apogee in the Cistercian Order, founded in 1098. Ornament was reduced to a Puritan minimum, liturgy was standardized, and rational planning was introduced into the running of abbeys. But the interest in reading and understanding Scripture that supported reform also paved the way for diverse interpretations of religious texts, especially among laymen. For, as numbers of readers and listeners grew, so, inevitably, did varieties of interpretation. Movements formed, attempted to institutionalize their ideas, and frequently came into conflict with the Church.

Before the age of printing the chief vehicle of communication used by both orthodox and unofficial groups was preaching. Nowadays, owing to the effects of printing, we are accustomed to think of preaching as an oral medium. But, during the Middle Ages and long afterwards, it was a means of conveying written material, chiefly the Bible, to less lettered and unlettered groups. Often sermons were delivered in local, vernacular languages, which made their message accessible to nonliterates. For the more learned, who had libraries and manuscripts, the spoken word could be supplemented by reading sermon collections, which furnished texts for personal meditation. But even among readers and writers of Latin, the sermon was inseparable from oral forms of composition and delivery, for which the medievals had ample stylebooks of rhetoric descending from Augustine's *De Doctrina Christiana*.

During the early Middle Ages, most preaching was done within the cloister. From the eleventh century on, public preaching became more common. Clerics like Robert of Arbrissel and Bernard of Tiron roamed the countryside of northern France, while, in Milan, one of Europe's first urban centers, the Patarene movement, which was in its early, ultra-orthodox stage, organized rallies of laymen and harangued crowds about the evils of simony and a married clergy. One of the most successful heterodox preachers of the twelfth century was Peter Waldo, the founder of the Waldensians, whose lifestyle of apostolic poverty foreshadowed the ideals of St. Francis. But there were many others—Vitalis of Savigny, Norbert of Xanten, and many nameless Cathars, as well as great reformist figures like Bernard of Clairvaux.

Orthodox preaching was encouraged by the tenth canon of the Fourth Lateran Council of 1215, which admonished bishops to preach publicly. This statement eventually led to the widespread preaching mission of the mendicant orders. But the spread of heresy via the spoken word and the text was also symptomatic of a major breakthrough in medieval communications. This was the free circulation of ideas, which was destined to play a large role in developing a skeptical, scientifically oriented view of the world. The West's earliest instrument of mass repression, the papal inquisition, was just as much a by-product of the new literacy, and began its unfortunate history under Gregory IX in 1233. What successfully challenged the Church's monopoly of religious literacy was the introduction, largely through preaching, of vernacular translations of the Bible. Vernacular literacy was a major issue in the Lollard movement, first in England and later under Jan Hus in Bohemia. The Hussite wars terminated with the agreement at Jihlava in 1436. It was little more than two generations later when Martin Luther presented his controversial theses in Wittenberg. The rebirth of literacy was not responsible for any of these changes, but it played an important role in shaping them all.

My second example of links between literacy and rationality moves to the inner life of the mind. It concerns the growth of interest in subjectivity and individuality after the eleventh century. We can also think of the change as a renewed concern with person and personality and with their links with community support and control.[24]

The change in sensibilities was widespread. In Abelard we witness a rebirth of autobiography. In Guibert of Nogent we have a memoir of deep conflict, in which the effective measure of time is personal experience. In Provençal poetry we revel in the emotional to-and-fro of the lover, who recreates the loved one to counterbalance his affective stance. In the mysticism of St. Bernard and William of St. Thierry another sort of subjectivity defines selfhood and otherness in religious language. The naturalism of Romanesque art and sculpture depends on the sensorium of the perceiver. The visual sense is everywhere extolled, both in scientific treatises and in the representation of fictional characters, who, like Alan of Lille's dreamers, literally read about the birth of the world and of man from Nature's garment. The period's literature is rich in mental processes—visions, statements about intentions, and musings on consciousness. The knights in Chrétien de Troyes' romances think, reflect, and attempt to link abstraction with moral action. In historical writing, the notion of an all-pervasive causality gives way to stories about the passions, motives, and instincts of human actors, as for instance in Orderic Vitalis's account of the founding of the Norman dynasty. In philosophy as well, subjectivity is expressed in a variety of ways: in theories of knowledge like Anselm's, which distinguish between *cogito* and *intellego*; or in notions of intentionality, which Abelard brings back to moral and ethical thought.

The list of potential examples is very long. The question is, how are we to understand what is taking place? Weber's approach to subjectivity will not do. As I have noted, it is not the strong point of his sociology.[25] Beyond that, the various activities and expressions cannot be divided into what he called means/end-rational, value-rational, affectual, and traditional orientations, since in Weber the diverse kinds of subjectivity and objectivity cut across other conceptual boundaries.[26]

The frontier he did not acknowledge is that which lies between orality and literacy. It is here that we find one of the sources of the new subjectivity. Europe had reached a new stage of cognitive development, which involved reading, writing, and audiences. Rationalities (I stress the plural) were linked to texts, which were everywhere interposed between experience and reality. The bookish culture was largely transmitted orally, but its reference system was the lexicon and the library. Furthermore, the process of rationalization only took place within the context of evolving relations between the spoken, the written, and the thought.

It is not rationality that produces literacy, for one can be rational without being self-consciously literate. But it is literacy, or the by-products of a culture of writing, that give medieval discussions of rationalization their peculiarly Western stamp. The object of thought is inseparable from the text that carries the sign of the thing; and texts, as a result, offer the dominant model for externalizing thought, in individuals as in groups.

As a consequence, the grammar of social relations is not a metaphor. It becomes a reality. It represents both the mental world and the structure of external events, since the conceptual filter for both is a text. The issues, as Hugh of St. Victor prudently observes, lie on the border of things, thoughts, and language. But it is here that we also see the type of rationality that in Weber's view has "the potential to introduce a methodical way of life"[27] based upon consistent ethical postulates. This rationality acts from within, and that is its link with the emerging subjectivity and individuality of medieval life and thought. But the dominant model is not economic rationality, as Weber thought. For this society has not sufficiently formalized thinking about the economy to look upon it as an independent variable. If there are ethically defensible principles for the activities of individuals and groups, they arise chiefly from the schemata of narratives that are heard or read.[28] Action is an audience reaction within a largely literary experience. This means that the design of activity, which is shaped as a narrative, is derived from the same texts that medieval culture produces as part of its literate revolution. Interiorization, the first stage of understanding something written, is also the primary phase of rationalization. It requires only that communication take place, that it be formalized subsequently by norms or rules, and that eventually it regulate key sectors of experience. In other words, contrary to what Weber proposed, substantive rationalization takes place by its own means and obeys its own criteria of change.

Weber recognized the role played by such forces as canon law, monasticism, and the Gregorian Reform in shaping medieval society. But, on the whole, he did not see in the Middle Ages the capacity for self-transformation that he associated with the innerworldly asceticism of the Reformation. The two ages were more alike than he thought. This becomes clear if we look at the public and private roles of penance.

By penance, I mean both the sacrament, which undergoes an internal evolution of its own, as well as a modeling process for behavior in secular society, for which penance provides a pattern. The key issue is not interiority, since inner repentance is essential in both public penance, which was introduced in the third century, and private penance, which made its initial appearance in the sixth. Rather, what changes is the relationship between inner and outer norms. As a consequence, there is an altered perception of the rationality behind public and private social conventions.

In public penance the penitent passed through a series of visible rituals of withdrawal and reintegration. He was either inside or outside the Christian community, which was a clearly defined microsociety in the later ancient and early medieval worlds. In private penance and, after the millennium, in secular penitential activities such as the pilgrimage or the crusade, there was an intermingling of collective rituals and individual reflection. Increasingly, in all activities affected by penance, the arbiter of one's destiny was one's own conscience. As one's inner mental processes became informed by the written word, the construction of the moral self was more and more a literary process. This was a religious and a secular transformation. In the sacrament, the individual had access from an early date to penitential books. From the twelfth century on, codified penitentials appeared, and, in the thirteenth, case-books of conscience. The manner of thinking developed in these treatises was reinforced by communities like confraternities and lay spiritual orders. In both the religious and the nonreligious spheres, the public and the private interacted in new ways that bound together the reasons why things were ethically right with the narrative shaping of lives in the image of that rightness.

Weber never denied that a type of rationality that oriented life patterns in an ethical manner was a fact of life in the Middle Ages. His theory of rationality makes a specific place for the value orientations of traditional society, just as his notion of ideal types provides a theoretical backdrop for their crystallization into behavioral patterns. However, he felt that only in the Reformation, and only under capitalism, were the values of implicit cultural narratives successfully challenged by the formal logic of the rationality of means and ends, whence his ambivalence on the ultimate benefits of modernization.

Was Weber right on this crucial question? The present state of research does not permit a definitive answer. No one disputes one issue: as far as we know, the language of economics was not used to formulate the problem of rationality during the early Middle Ages, as it was increasingly after the thirteenth century. On all other issues, the bulk of the evidence suggests that the pre-Reformation period was essentially in continuity with what came afterwards. In the case of subjectivity and individualism, we see the appearance of new sensibilities at an early date. The eleventh century saw the rise of an ethical and substantive rationality based on literary precedents and largely in harmony with tradition. The period also witnessed the creation of more objectively perceived rationalities, sometimes bearing ethical connotations, in the political and military spheres. Genuine political theory emerges in John of Salisbury and later in Marsilius of Padua. Militaristic and colonial ideologies also appear.

My illustrations—dissent, subjectivity, and penance—do not

exhaust the potential of medieval evidence for an examination of Weberian and post-Weberian ideas on rationality. They are only examples. If a full review of the issues were attempted, other questions would have to be raised. One of these is the change Weber identified as disenchantment (*Entzauberung*). By this, Weber meant, not a state of mind, but a process, a literal de-magification or dis-enchanting.[29] He recommended a historical inquiry of this type on several occasions, but he never actually pursued it using Western sources. The Reformation chapter was sketched, but as Hans Liebeschütz notes, Weber "never executed his project of studying the impact of biblical rationalism on the structure of thought and action in the Middle Ages."[30] Once again, we face the problem of Weberian scholarship catching up with medieval research. The "desacralization" of the medieval universe has been actively studied since the pioneering work of M.-D. Chenu.[31] It remains for this newly published and recently discussed corpus of medieval texts to be integrated into the developmental theory of rationalization.

This topic arises from within medieval culture. Others require a comparative perspective. Literacy was not a uniquely Christian phenomenon in the Middle Ages. Oral and written discourse were also common to medieval Judaism and Islam. What is characteristic of these three religions is their scriptural foundation. What is different is the manner in which the scriptural element is translated into institutions. One of Weber's merits was to have drawn attention to the value of the Hebraic moral outlook in the development of Western rationalization, however misguided some of his conceptions of ancient Jewish society and culture.[32] Weber devoted his attention to the episodes in the history of rationality that particularly interested him, such as the end of the ancient world and the Reformation. But, as F. H. Tenbruck notes, "the intermediary stages remain relatively undefined."[33]

A basic problem arises from the concept of Scripture itself. In the popular imagination, the notion conjures up the image of something written. Yet in Judaism, Christianity, and Islam, the transcription of God's word is looked upon as a mere aide-mémoire. The experience of Scripture is oral and aural. Hence, in the three religions of the book, there is an interplay of orality and literacy. Where they differ is in their hermeneutics. For Judaism, as Jacob Neusner points out, a critical phase begins with the Mishnah, a philosophical law code written about A.D. 200, and concludes with the Talmud of Babylonia in A.D. 600.[34] In Islam, by contrast, there was from the outset "a generic concept of scripture." But paradoxically, Islam is closer than either Judaism or Christianity to treating scripture as the "verbatim speech of God."[35] In Christianity the process of rationalization is part of the evolving tradition of oral and written religious discourse. Whereas Judaism and Islam maintained religious hermeneutics as an isolated sphere of thought, Christianity began the dialogue with modernity in which Weber rightly saw the origins of the "economic ethics" of religion.

I conclude by reminding the reader that I set as my task an immanent critique of rationality as it arose in medieval society and thought. By this I mean a criticism that grows naturally out of the conditions of understanding of the Middle Ages. But it is important to distinguish between a critique of modernization and rationalization and an ideology of antimodernism. Weber never fell into this intellectual trap. Like Tönnies, Simmel, and Sombart, but with a unique clarity of vision, Weber saw that rationalization could bring about either freedom in society or a new type of enslavement. Precisely this view developed in the Middle Ages. It was not directed, as were Weber's observations, at the limitations formal rationality places on individuals in industrial, bureaucratic society, but at the illusion of freedom created by textual, scholastic, and legally defined cultural norms. By the fourteenth century the medievals had few illusions about the truths of texts. They were also skeptical about circular thinking in hermeneutics. Anselm, Thomas Aquinas, and William of Ockham, differing on much else, are agreed in pointing out the limits of reason—that is, of textually established rationalites. It is here, as well as in the more fashionable opposition of heretics, that one finds an internal critique of medieval society and its nascent rationality. The Middle Ages are the period in which we can trace the forerunners of rationalization processes, as Weber suspected. More important, they were a time in which the debate about rationality began in a recognizably modern culture. To tell this story accurately, and without polemics, is to complete Weber's program. That is the challenge.

CHAPTER SEVEN

TEXTUAL COMMUNITIES: JUDAISM, CHRISTIANITY, AND THE DEFINITIONAL PROBLEM

As discussed in this volume, there are essentially two sides to the question of literacy and society. One is theoretical, the other, practical. I have drawn attention to a neglected dimension of social theory, particularly in Max Weber. I have also suggested ways in which the study of early orality and literacy can help us to understand many of the assumptions that underpin contemporary communications.

This essay develops these themes further. In the first part, questions are raised about the notion of a textual community: what its theoretical background is, why literacy is not textuality, and how we can distinguish composition and context in historical perspective. In the second part I turn to a practical issue. I ask whether the concept of the textual community, which was invented to deal with medieval evidence, can clarify the religious changes of the first six centuries after Christ, and how it must be modified if it is to do so.

I

I begin with a little background. The contemporary study of oral and written culture is about a century old—older if one takes account of its links with the beginnings of modern hermeneutics in Schleiermacher. It has evolved as an interdisciplinary field, but one in which, for better or worse, there is no central discipline. The oralities and literacies of the past are regularly made the subject of inquiries by linguists, philosophers, theologians, anthropologists, and historians. But there is no common methodology, and the methods developed in one discipline are not always recognized in others.

The original inspiration for the study of the social function of texts came from classical sociology, but the momentum of research has been taken over by anthropology. It was a short step from the search in Marx, Weber, and Durkheim for the ideas behind social changes to the investigation of the means of communication by which ideas are transmitted from one generation to the next. A parallel in early economic history linked rising literacy to modernization and social progress.

From the outset, anthropologists and ethnographers saw matters differently. They were normally face to face with living nonliterate peoples, none of whom seemed to be nonliterate in precisely the same way. From such studies arose the first decentering insight into literacy: namely, that it is not one thing, but many things loosely grouped under a modernist rubric.

Historians, who have developed low-level generalizations about orality and literacy, have usually done so from the archival equivalent of fieldwork. Not surprisingly, what we have in anthropology and history is a cluster of synthetic ideas based on observed regularities in which there is a healthy scope for regional and linguistic variety. Some researchers question whether we can go any further than this. All recognize that what one is entitled to ask depends on the type of society one is studying. For instance, we can ask whether an authentically oral outlook permeates the *Chanson de Roland*, whose memorable verses were first transcribed during a revival of literate education. But the question must be asked differently of a work like the *Satyricon* of Petronius, even though it is rich in actual speech, for during the first century A.D., literate expectations in society were the norm.

Again, we can speak of separate traditions of the oral and the written, which may correspond to different views of reality. In China, written language establishes common meanings, while different pronunciations occur in a large number of spoken languages. In early European history, there is a less radical, but nonetheless perceptible, separation between the spoken and the written in Ireland, Merovingian Gaul, and Iceland. By contrast, among the scattered religious communities of late antiquity and the nascent Middle Ages, there is a common assumption that reality lies behind the written language of Scripture. The oral and the written are accordingly seen as strategies of expression, not as means of social definition.

In short, the first lesson that anthropology and history teach us about literacy is this: if cultures are comparable, they are also different.

But, if they are different, they are also comparable. And they develop over time. Early theorists knew this, but they did not always react with subtlety. The study of communications was greatly oversimplified. One can classify the naive approaches in several ways. For some, "oral" and "written" seemed to mark inviolable boundaries in the evolution of culture. Others admired orality or literacy for their own sake. On the one side there were the Romantics, who looked back nostalgically to an oral utopia before the appearance of the mentally and morally crippling vice of script. This view lies behind many fascist attempts to define the *Volk*, as well as less offensive folklore theories of primitive culture. One also finds an element of it in perceptions of "prescripsarian" tribal paradises from Rousseau to Lévi-Strauss.

Through such schemas, as noted, oral and written took their place alongside other global concepts like traditional and modern, prelogical and logical, and magical and scientific. The vocabulary of orality and literacy superseded some of these approaches because it carried a less burdensome ideological baggage. But one can question whether it added up to much of an advance. On the one hand, relativizers could argue that orality and literacy merely divided culture in a new way into haves and have-nots. Literacy, rationality, and modernity were roughly equated, and the literacy myth succeeded the former narratives of Western progress. Needless to say, this playing with categories dramatically falsified historical realities. It also contaminated the terms innocently employed by empirical researchers. Jack Goody, commenting on the rigidities in the field, remarks sagely that the framework for understanding was "either non-developmental or simplistically so."[1]

Even if these educated prejudices are overcome, the historian who wishes to use the notion of literacy faces another issue. This is the ambivalence of the concept itself. As a developmental idea, it is heavily weighted in favor of what Harold Innis aptly terms "the bias of communication,"[2] which always places the operational vocabulary in the hands of the survivors of an evolutionary process. So it is with literacy. The normal use of the term is restrictive: the analysis is limited to the routines of a culture that took shape in the later ancient world and the Middle Ages, and reached a mechanically reproducible stage in the age of print. Let us not entertain illusions about impartial observers or value-neutral languages in the social sciences. To write up a culture is to create it in a sense, and this is always done from someone's point of view. There may be no entirely satisfactory way of counterbalancing this ideological tonnage.[3]

There is one potential way around the problem: not to use *literacy* (and, by implication *orality*), in an unqualified manner. We have other words that adequately describe what is taking place.

During the 1960s it became fashionable for students of literature to speak of *textuality*. The idea was not new, except in the emphasis on breaking with earlier critical language, and, among structuralists, in the effort to replace diachrony with synchrony. As a stabilizer for the concept of literacy, textuality has certain advantages. For, when we talk of literacy, we often mean the uses of texts, and it is here that a confusion arises. This is because literacy is a generic term of reference, or poses as one, while the uses of texts are historically specific.

The two notions are also dissimilar in other respects that potentially contribute to historical analysis. This becomes evident, if we consider, not what texts are, but what people do with them. Literates can do without actual texts and yet remain a part of the world of reading and writing. Literates do not carry libraries with them; they transform a lot of what they know into procedural memory, so that actions based ultimately on texts appear to be automatic. At the other end of the spectrum, nonliterates utilize texts for causative functions that have nothing to do with the writing they contain. Among unlettered peasants in the Middle Ages, the presence of parchment without any legal text often created exactly the same effect as a drawn-up contract for labor and services. Even literates behave this way: The Greek phylactery, the Latin amulet, the Arab ḥirz, and the Jewish kemi'a all symbolize, but do not state, religious obligations.[4] Clearly there are types of literacy that do not demand specific texts, just as there are magical textualities that work among nonliterates.

There is also textuality that works orally. Were the memorizers of the oral Torah in antiquity nonliterates, or were they merely dispensing with the need for writing? Obviously there is something more at work here than mere orality. Otherwise there would have been no reason for the gradual shift from the oral to the written Torah that took place between A.D. 200 and 600. The movement toward the written text within an already highly literate group must be seen against the background of social and historical factors, but above all as a response to changes in communication itself. A potent force was the rise of a somewhat different textual tradition in Christianity, as well as the presence of other scripturalist sects, such as the Manicheans. Conversely, Christian textuality, which is not foreshadowed in the gospels, was doubtless a reaction to an already developing process of change within the oral and written traditions of Judaism, as St. Paul suggests in his calculated jibes about the letter and the spirit. In content of doctrine, the two religions were soon independent; in means of communication, they developed interdependently.

In Western development, this is the typical situation. Oral and written traditions normally function in relation to each other. They influence each other, overtly and covertly, within institutions and between institutions. As noted, some students of the issues are emotionally committed to the idea that cultures have to be oral *or* written. This is sometimes the case, but normally not in the West. During the Middle Ages, the high point of orality after archaic Greece and Mesopotamia, texts almost vanished from view, but never the model or memory of them, which continued to guide expression and behavior through the so-called Dark Ages (whose darkness is merely a metaphor for the disappearance of writing). The written word did not rule *in absentia*, nor the spoken *in praesentia*. They governed together, and this fact must be remembered despite the oral or written traditions provided by different disciplines such as literature and law. There is variety in the way in which traditions evolved, but there is a common frame of reference.

One element that must be reckoned with in any discussion of the history of orality and literacy is self-consciousness, in particular the consciousness of change. The subjective awareness of change is a potent factor in bringing about new ways of looking at things. It is also one of their most obvious consequences. In the early Middle Ages, rituals and oral traditions were public. There was little search for inner meaning, hence no trouble was taken to record rituals in writing. In the later Middle Ages, people became just as convinced that an interior sense lurked behind every outer expression or behavioral pattern. It was this belief in the interior nature of meaning, as well as the formation of programs of action based on the linking up of individual cases of interiority, that brought about change as often as real shifts in communications. There is no doubt that the rise of this idea paralleled the growth of a more literate society. For the written word was the symbol of the inner, often unconscious, and divinely or diabolically inspired network of sense. Out of this arose the desire for a grammar that could accommodate both literary and social relations.

The element that allows us to study this type of change effectively is not literacy but textuality. What we inquire into is the specific uses of texts: who uses them, and why. Texts, I add, are both physical and mental. The "text" is what a community takes it to be. Texts have propositional content, but they are procedural knowledge. For, like meaning in language, the element a society fixes upon is a conventional arrangement among the members. If there is such a thing as a purely abstract notion of a text, it has to be one that is easily adapted to a wide variety of actual circumstances. This does not mean that the charters of communities are interchangeable, only that all have some way of registering semantic and social relations that are understandable to the speakers, listeners, readers, and writers. In the oral society of the early Middle Ages, the text is internal: it is what the actors understand by public rituals. If they did not comprehend some meaning in common, the ritual would have no force. By contrast, in the later Middle Ages and the early modern world, texts are normally physical and visible, but they are thought to have inner logic and sense. Oral society has faith in one type of text, literate society in another.

My deliberate opaqueness on this issue parallels certain gnomic formulations in the later Wittgenstein, especially the idea that meaning is public and conventional.[5] But there is a difference between what I have in mind and what philosophers of language talk about. Philosophy does not normally use the terms *oral* and *written*. If one takes the long view, an opportunity would appear to have been lost. For the question of the spoken and its status with respect to fixed meaning is in the mainstream of thinking about language in Plato and Aristotle. The shape of the discussion changed in the Middle Ages, when Scripture was a major concern of thinkers, and again after the age of print, which established a secular scripturalism in the West. But the basic features are still alive in the classic hermeneutic balance of Kant. It was after the eighteenth century that something went wrong. Richard Rorty claims that philosophy gradually lost its ability to act as a foundation for the cultural disciplines.[6] If this is partly true, then one reason may be found in the contemporary separation of the inquiry into meaning from the means of communication. There is a weak reflection of this concern in the debate over whether the voice or writing officiates in the original creation of sense. But this is not the same as asking how text formation takes place and how texts interact with society.

There is another distinction in the field that is related to these issues. One can speak of orality and literacy in literary or philosophical terms, and one can study a set of social and historical relationships. But these are not the same. In the one case, the emphasis is inevitably compositional; in the other, it is contextual. Let me explain.

To look at composition is to ask how oral and written records came into being. The oral or written text is the end point of the investigation. We can ask how Homer, the Torah, the gospels, *Beowulf*, or Slavic epics were composed and performed; or, like Bakhtin, we can see a more general problem in speech genres—that is, in "the selection of the lexical, phraseological, and grammatical resources of the language, but above all through their compositional structure."[7] Composition and performance are social acts, as are drama, dialogue, and interaction rituals. But here, feedback works mainly between the actor and the world of his or her utterance. Composition can also tell us about the relation between the oral and the written, as does Werner Kelber's *The Oral and the Written Gospel.*[8] In general, the compositional emphasis has favored the oral: the recovery of the oral literatures of non-Western peoples, or, in criticism, the uncovering of the rhythmical elements of poetics.

The other approach is contextual. Here, feedback works differently. We are no longer dealing with the creation of ideas or expressions, or with psychological questions that historians cannot answer. The individual who creates a work and the work as created object have socially definable careers over time. They can be studied through the reactions others have to them. There is also a reorientation of intentions. The originator's intentions are unknowable, but the work's intentions can be analyzed in its internal structure or in its describable effects, which are a part of its history. One of the assumptions of the contextual approach is that in a society the transition to a new set of working relations between oral and written culture is a potent force for change in two historical senses: it shapes real changes and it shapes the modes of thought by which change is understood and interpreted.

II

So far, I have argued that one of the ways in which societies differ is in the way groups within them conceptualize internal relations between the oral and the written. There is a narrative logic in these responses that can transcend social, economic, or political bonds. If the self-definition of one group is through writing, it is in the nature of things that the opposite party will think of themselves as directed toward the oral, unspoken, or spontaneous. Thus, as a facet of discourse, the alleged literalism of the ancient Jew helped to produce the oral orientation of the Christian. The existence of the Christian in turn helped Judaism to define itself.

But there is a problem with this way of looking at relations between the two religions. They are both scriptural, and yet they both envisage themselves as obeying the word of God.

What kind of "word" is this? In large part, it is a metaphor that uses orality to describe interchanges between God and man. In monotheism it is necessary to establish a direct link between the authority behind Scripture and the obligations of man. This type of oral bond is compositional: it relates the intentions of the creator to the actions of his creature. However, when the believers of a monotheistic faith turn to the task of interpretation, it is necessary to adopt a contextualist approach. The gymnastics of verbalism aside, the adepts all arrive at meaning through a reading of the Hebrew Bible or the New Testament. Those enlightened directly by God can receive his words in a variety of ways. But the rest of us, as Augustine observed, have to read the transcript.[9] Only in this way can words play their ambivalent role in Judaism and Christianity, at once looking back nostalgically to an atemporal mode and looking forward to the inevitable constitution of canon and tradition, by which ecclesiastical institutions influence the lives of real men and women. In Judaism, this textual panoply became central after the destruction of the temple cult in A.D. 70. For Christianity, it is implicit in the communicative strategy that privileges the spirit of the text as the essential bonding of God and man.

The metaphors of orality do not end with the original creation of the text. They are reinvigorated each time Scripture is read. The ritual of reading recapitulates the primal experience of speaking and hearing the word of God. Each reading is a speaking anew. But the reality of scriptural knowledge is established contextually by believers who arrive on the scene *post textum*. For them, faith may be in the word, but proof is in the text. This is true for Scriptures that are actually read as well as for those that are memorized and recited, such as the oral gospels and the oral Torah. This recall is a type of rereading.

But wherever there are such texts, there is the possibility of textual communities.

We can think of a textual community as a group that arises somewhere in the interstices between the imposition of the written word and the articulation of a certain type of social organization. It is an interpretive community, but it is also a social entity.

The basic components of the textual community have been mentioned earlier in this volume.[10] I summarize them here. Wherever there are texts that are read aloud or silently, there are groups of listeners that can potentially profit from them. A natural process of education takes place within the group, and, if the force of the word is strong enough, it can supersede the differing economic and social backgrounds of the participants, welding them, for a time at least, into a unit. In other words, the people who enter the group are not precisely the same as those who come out. Something has happened, and this experience affects their relations both with other members and with those in the outside world. Among the members, solidarity prevails, with the outside, separation. The members may disperse, but they can also institutionalize their new relations, for instance, by forming a religious order or a sectarian movement that meets on regular occasions. If they take this course, the community acquires the ability to perpetuate itself. An aspect of the social lives of the group's members will from that moment be determined by the rules of membership in the community. There has to be a common understanding of these guidelines, as well as mechanisms for interpretation and transmission. The Scriptures are not the rules: there is a difference in form and content between the Torah and the Mishnah, and between the monastic prescriptions of the New Testament and the Rule of St. Benedict. It is the rules, not the Scriptures, that transcend preexisting economic or social bonds, since it is the rules that are both the basis and the result of common interpretive efforts. These rules democratize life in a sense, since one can put aside the past. What the Mishnah says applies equally to rich and poor. So do the *dicta* of the monks.

But there is a problem in applying the notion of the textual community directly to ancient evidence. The idea was invented to interpret the beliefs and activities of small, isolated, heretical and reformist groups in medieval Europe. Its members were not great prophets: they were usually marginal men and women, sectarians, schismatics, preachers, and practitioners of magic. In analysing their activity, the main context of experience is the experience of the text. In antiquity, conditions were different. Above all, in a society in which literacy was routine, more attention must be paid to reception and reader reconstruction, to intertextuality, and to oral discourse within well-worn rhetorical channels. One must also deal with canon and authority.

There are therefore good reasons to modify the original scheme. One is to counter the notion that the textual community is a philosophical abstraction rather than a working conceptualization. Another arises from the recognition that we are dealing with a different sort of text. In medieval communities, inasmuch as nonliteracy was the rule, the texts were short, simple in message, and not deeply contextualized. But contrast, in antiquity, when an educated community was assumed, the writings were longer, more complicated, and inseparable from their historical contexts.

As a consequence, in the Middle Ages, the text often started up the community. In antiquity, the community preceded the critical text, which might bring about reform, reorganization, or sectarianism. This means that in ancient groups there was an already-existing self-conscious tradition. The coalescing of a new text is seen as a chapter in an ongoing narrative. The history of the Jews does not begin with the Mishnah, nor that of the Christians with the desert fathers. Contexts exist; and they have the potential to transcend textual communities, as churches inevitably consolidate their identification with the narratives of which they are a part.

Rather than community alone, I would prefer to typify these groups as combinations of narratives, in which the actor's role is much like the dramatic performance of a script. (In my view, medieval drama bridges the gap between the oral and the written in a similar way.) In this narrative, it is not a text but life that is seen as a story. It has a beginning, a middle, and an end, a climax and a denouement. The shape of the story is aesthetically coherent, allowing for the response that completes what Roman Ingarden calls the artistic pole of the reading process,[11] and what I call the contextual counterpart of the compositional mode. The shaping devices produce in life the rough equivalents of the rhetorical strategies of storytelling, such as metaphor and irony, tropes that permit the typifying of elements in the narrative.[12]

In Judaism and Christianity, there is also an ethical dimension to the story. Aesthetic coherence thereby becomes associated in the members' minds with ethical rightness. The compositional component of the experience is the living out of respective ethnic histories and the ritualistic displaying of covenants between man and God. But, because this orality is only known through texts, reading is an endowing of principles with values for life situations. The link between reading and behavior is direct, no matter how it is conceptualized in the words of men or of God. We thereby find in the textual community—which, in this instance, may comprise the whole of a people—a way of completing the picture of ethical categories and subjective human action discussed by Max Weber. Ethical rightness appears to the actors to be a rationale for thought and action: it is the means by which individuals explain the why of patterned events to themselves. Material factors are not excluded from the process of decision-making, but they have no particular priority. What is essential is a subjectively perceived and intertextually supported rightness of conduct. We can say that the members of such a community will, intend, project, and shape their futures. Based on the commonly held rules of the group, they think they are guiding their courses of action, and this thinking conspires with events to give a sense of order and direction to what they do. So conceived, the textual community introduces a new level of ritual into everyday life. Individuals may still adhere to ceremonies and routines that antedate their membership. Also, it should be noted that these rituals affect critical aspects of decision-making, not the experience of life as a whole, which contains many nonreflective elements. But ritual is different before and after the introduction of texts, and here arises another theoretical question that must be addressed.

Ritual is an indispensable term of analysis in social research, but it is notoriously difficult to define. Victor Turner, building on the insights of Arnold van Gennep, sees in the theory of ritual a means of describing many of the root forms of symbolic behavior in society. Judaism and Christianity, and, even more emphatically, Islam furnish examples of the all-encompassing rituals Turner analyses (see ch. 4, n. 14). The notions of liminality and *communitas* are particularly useful tools of discussion, since they owe their origin to medieval patterns of activity. Yet Turner's ideas are mainly applicable at a macrosociological level. They are much less help in microsociology, which is the natural domain of the textual community. For such groups normally see themselves as small units within the whole: they are the dissenters and reformers, whose social dramas are played out against the backdrop of a larger world.

Another limitation of the notion of ritual derives from the anthropological approach as a whole. In general, the term *ritual* refers to the oral-aural dimension of communication. This demotes all activity for which there is a set of written rules. These are mere ceremonies. In my view, if the notion of ritual is to help us understand early Christian and Jewish life, we have to avoid this privileging of the oral mode. For it implies that much ritual is procedural or unconscious, and thus unavailable for historical analysis. The most helpful pointer for understanding how ritual functions within textual communities comes from Erving Goffman's studies of interaction among the members of institutions for which there are, if not written, at least implicit rules for behavior.[13] What would happen, I ask, if such guidelines were made explicit by means of a text? We would arrive at a rather different notion of ritual, one that involves interaction with a script in a group attempting to achieve a new balance between inherited written and creative oral tradition. The orality of this rule-oriented ritual is what gave shape to the routines of rabbinic Judaism and the spoken gospel narratives.

Something should be said here about a phenomenon common to both the community and the rituals. This is historicization. Innovation in religious groups takes place in the present, but the moment writings enter the picture, the community acquires a historical dimension. Both perspectives on what is happening are valid. For the founders of a new group, the breakthrough to a different way of looking at things is an unprecedented event. For later adherents, or for the same adherents later on, the strains of creating a movement may be less evident. Links can then be forged with the traditional teachings that the founders challenged. Sometimes this is done by comparing a disfavored past with a present of utopian potential, as when Augustine completed the transformation of salvation-oriented Christianity into a polity for running the church and the state. In Judaism, as continuity is more important than discontinuity, there is a somewhat different scenario for achieving aesthetic distance in the Tosefta, the Yerushalmi, and the Bavli.

But Jews and Christians are similar inasmuch as both exhibit attitudes toward a past that is configured in writings. In Judaism between the second and the sixth centuries, much of the reconciliation of opposing views—the Torah with the Mishnah, the Mishnah in turn with various exegetical collections—took place in the forum of oral discussion and debate. In Christianity during the same formative centuries, we observe developments at both interpretive and institutional levels. Tradition, especially after Tertullian, came to be represented by a body of dogma and by the living Church, with its legal and administrative setup. The oral element, which in Judaism is a debate between sages, is elevated neoplatonically beyond the range of the mundane business affairs of synods. In both religions a living text succeeds combinations of traditional written and contemporaneous oral ones. There is no equivalent in Judaism of the Church, just as there is no parallel in Christianity for the rabbi, who is the "living Torah."[14]

There are other differences between the two. In Judaism, as Jacob Neusner illustrates, the two media were embodied in the two Torahs, the one written, the other spoken and memorized. When the authors of the Mishnah began the process of writing out the oral Torah around A.D. 200, they formed a loosely coordinated textual community. But it differed from other groups of this type. First, its oral recollection was really a type of literacy: it was a rereading based on remembering what had been recorded. Also, the rabbis had a clearly defined, authoritative canon of texts behind them. The Mishnah was nonetheless a turning-point. Although the process of writing continued down to around A.D. 600 in the Bavli, the composition of the Mishnah was the event in which the horizontal energies of group consciousness, essential for a community, interacted with the vertical energies of tradition. For "the Mishnah referred to nothing prior to itself—except (and then, most implicitly and by indirection) to Scripture."[15] One line of interpretation led from the Mishnah to the Yerushalmi and the Bavli, while another formed three separate branches of exegesis, dealing respectively with the Mishnah, with Scripture, and with theological problems arising from Jewish tradition. Each of these developments has its own milieu and history. But they are not all textual communities, since the differing interpretations do not issue in rule-bound patterns of behavior that break with what has come before. They are reading or interpretive communities, whose purpose is to follow the hermeneutic path of reintegrating "new horizons" with the old.

By contrast, early Christianity had no Torah. The offshoot of Judaism was not able to build on a hard literary tradition from within that was different from its source until the New Testament achieved a canonical authority equal to the Hebrew Bible. Yet the problem of group belief and practice entered a new phase during the lifetime of St. Paul. Clearly, forces were at work.

But what forces? Although parallels should not be pushed too far, some features of Pauline Christianity appear to have anticipated what happened in medieval sects. In both cases, explanation has favored two theses. One looks for common elements in the social background of the members, and seeks to relate beliefs to their intellectual environments. The other regards beliefs themselves as the determining force behind early Christianity, and looks upon religion as an autonomous aspect of cultural development. In his authoritative study of the field, Wayne Meeks analyzes the various interpretations and finds them unsatisfactory.[16] One cannot trace the uniqueness of Paul's followers to their social background or belief structures alone. Like medieval dissenters the Christian converts who met in different imperial towns and listened to Paul appear to have come from no single stratum of society. No sex, economic level, or professional calling predominates. Rather, the people "of several social levels are brought together."[17] Also, like medieval reformers, they show broad divergencies in interpreting the central doctrines of the new faith. These are reflected in their methods of governing themselves and in their rites of worship.

Yet there was a common experience, the urban association of the *ekklēsia,* which, Meeks shows, differed from other types of social organization such as the household, the *collegium*, the synagogue, and the school. But is this all? I would suggest a further element: the textually organized education of the members in the groups, which effectively transcended their backgrounds, professional allegiances, and antecedent beliefs. It was not the urban environment that was the cause of this experience: this was merely the setting in which the members conveniently met, were initiated into the cult, and returned to their ordinary lives. Like all textual communities, the Christian *ekklēsia* did not affect all areas of life and thought: it chiefly brought about a break with tradition in a few critical areas. Also, this reorientation of belief was played out as a drama in which the oral confronted the written. Paul never tires of telling his followers of the advantages of the spirit over the letter, or of emphasizing the doctrine of charity by which the Word is transformed into behavior toward one's neighbors, friends, associates, and even oneself. Finally, self-consciousness had a large role. The Christians may not have been very different from the Jews of their time in the urban existence they led. But they thought they were different, and this conceptualization was the grounding of a script on which the community based its behavior.

As I originally conceived the notion of the textual community, it was intended to fill a theoretical gap in the conception of Church and sect as outlined by Ernst Troeltsch and deepened by Max Weber. As these pioneers knew, early Christians were natural candidates for such an approach, since ancient sources define the group as a sect within Judaism. The weakness of their theory was to leave no middle ground between the institutional notion of the Church and the anarchic anti-structure of the sect. Also, they failed to reckon with the fact that what one believes is shaped by the means of communication by which the content is transmitted. The mere application of the concept of a textual community to early Christian life and thought is no overall solution to these difficulties. But is has advantages over early approaches in one respect. It allows that the most important influences on forming the ideas that make a group cohere are those that take place among the group's members during the processes of conversion, initiation, and confirmation. These are the rituals of self-definition. Such experiences can be replicated, as they were wherever Paul spoke. But each group must undergo the rite of passage on its own.

These illustrations based on the work of authorities in other fields are not meant to do disservice to ideas that may not harmonize with my own. I only wish to draw attention to similarities where they unquestionably exist. Even on the basis of such limited examples, I would suggest that the study of orality and literacy promises some unusual perspectives on long-debated issues. I also propose in the next chapter that this approach can help us reassess the role of tradition itself. Jewish and Christian ideas of tradition are close, but far from identical. One reason for their dissimilarity lies in their ways of dealing with texts and textuality. There is a common ground in the recognition of a difference between tradition perceived as past practices and as present applications of what was done in the past. Neither the ancient Jews nor the Christians went back to the Bible to find anything as abstract as the idea of tradition. Rather they did so to locate precise texts that justified, authenticated, and legitimized different types of group experience. Tradition became the interpretation of traditions. As time went on, the boundaries grew. Judaism reached the stage of continuity between a textual past and present by the sixth century. Christianity did not do so until several centuries later, some would say in the thirteenth century, others not until the sixteenth. One of the problems awaiting historians is to sort out the role that speaking, listening, reading, and writing played in shaping attitudes toward the living past.

CHAPTER EIGHT

TRADITION AND MODERNITY: MODELS FROM THE PAST

Tradition and modernity are the most troubling concepts in cultural analysis. We are never quite sure what they mean. The sense we give to modernity depends to some degree on what we think of as tradition. One society's traditions can easily become another's modernity, like the venerable African masks that occasionally inspired the cubist art of Braque and Picasso.

The field of study is also somewhat unbalanced. There are dozens of works on modernity, and many more if one includes related notions like modernism, modernization, and postmodernism. There are far fewer inquiries into the nature of tradition, and few indeed that have a theoretical dimension. S. N. Eisenstadt, Edward Shils, and J. C. Heesterman[1] have attempted to reverse this trend. But they remain exceptions to the general neglect of tradition among social scientists.

The negative feelings about tradition have historical roots. Since the Enlightenment, *tradition* and *change* have generally been looked upon as opposites. The term normally applied to social, economic, or cultural transformations is *modernity*. Most post-Enlightenment philosophies equate modernity and change. The connection entered the social sciences via Kant and Hegel, and we find it reproduced in a similar fashion by thinkers as diverse in establishing reasons for change as Marx, Durkheim, and Weber. With modernity identified with change, and by implication with the positive values associated with progress, tradition automatically came to mean the culturally changeless and historically immobile. In classical sociological theory, tradition is most easily defined as the stage of society from which we all emerged. In the eighteenth century, this usually meant the Middle Ages; in the nineteenth century and twentieth, it has also come to mean primitive, non-Western societies.

Since the nineteenth century, when medieval studies was recognized as a branch of professional historical inquiry, medievalists have reacted strongly against the view that theirs was a period of social or cultural immobility. In general, the discipline adopted the opposite ideology. The defense of their age as a period of progressive change has created an emotional bond among medievalists who often have little else in common.

Demonstrations of medieval "modernity" have multiplied in our time. The theses in the field are so numerous that they hardly merit extensive review. Among popular books, one thinks of Jacques Le Goff's *Les intellectuels au moyen âge* (1957), Eugène Vinaver's *The Rise of Romance* (1972), and Colin Morris's *The Discovery of the Individual* (1972). The term *modernus* and the rare substantive *modernitas* have been the subject of inquiries by M.-D. Chenu, E. R. Curtius, Edouard Jeauneau, Hubert Silvestre, W. Hartmann, and Elisabeth Gössmann.[2] In the background stands a larger modernizing thesis, that of the renaissance of the twelfth century.[3] The details of such studies vary, but the message is the same. They say that the Middle Ages were a time of change, of incipient modernity. Change is modernity, modernity is change. And, to most historians, this seems to be the way things should be.

There is nothing wrong with this approach, except that it leaves the concept of tradition in limbo. For, in this way of looking at things, modernity can have many facets, but tradition only one. Oddly enough, this narrowing of perspective is not only typical of studies of medieval modernity. One also finds it in books that lodge their values in tradition, such as were popular in Germany and France during the 1930s. In order to serve their ideological purposes too, tradition was viewed as a monolith. Just as medievalists have established paradigms of change in the Middle Ages, they have helped to create the myth of medieval tradition as a reference point for immobile values.[4]

But is tradition immobile? I think not. A great deal depends on what we mean by tradition. This is what we have not sorted out, either as medievalists or as theorists of culture.

In agreement with Edward Shils, Jerzy Szacki, and Martin Krygier,[5] I would propose that there are at least three elements in tradition that should be included in any discussion of culture and institutions. These are pastness, authoritative presence, and the means of transmission.

Traditions may not be very old, and they can be invented for economic or political motives.[6] Yet for traditionalism to work, they must be perceived as belonging to the past. They are part of a narrative of social development that begins in the past and leads to the present. As regards the rationalities that affect decision-making, this means that the past carries greater weight than the present. The past influences, even determines, what is to be done now and in the future. The past can harbor diverse beliefs, values, and motives. However, in traditional thinking, such differences are minimized. Tradition bestows on past experience an overriding sense of unity.

Yet if traditions are past, they are also present. This presentness can be embodied in a charismatic prophet or represented in the institutions of law and government. It can work through the author of a single text, a holy book, or through the more mundane accumulation of codes and archives.[7] Through the human or artificial memory of the past, tradition holds the present in its grasp. Of course, traditions refer to what really took place as well as to much that did not. Arthurian legends and ideas of courtly love both inspired behavioral reactions in the fourteenth century, but it is doubtful if either referred back to actual social practices. I should add, not necessarily in a Lacanian sense, that the past can function without an authoritative presence via the unconscious. One thinks of taboos, kinship rules, and some purificatory rituals.

Finally, for traditions to be operative in society, they must be transmitted. There is not only a *traditum;* there is also a *traditio.* In the Middle Ages, this means by oral, written, or visual communication. The type of transmission is not neutral: it is rooted in politics and institutions, and it helps to shape the message it transmits. The manner in which a tradition is handed over from one generation to the next is a clue to its place in the social fabric and to the source of its legitimizing power. It also tells us something about the relation of forms of community behavior over time. In an age of record-keeping, incipient bureaucracy, and written law like the early thirteenth century, the oral transmission of feudal rights and ritualized gift-giving meant something different from what they meant two centuries earlier. For in a society that acknowledges the authority of written communication, those who record and edit the past have a means of controlling the future that is inaccessible to nonliterates.[8] In these circumstances, the act of writing up a society's past is tantamount to recreating its culture.[9]

There is one other feature of tradition that I think important for understanding the Middle Ages, although it is not often mentioned in the standard accounts of the subject. This is the geographical dimension. The coalescing of a tradition often corresponds to the settlement and organization of a society within definable geographical boundaries, for which the writing down of traditions acts like a set of intellectual fenceposts. The Visigothic, Frankish, and other Germanic law codes in the early Middle Ages can be viewed in this light; and, in a similar sense we speak of Anglo-Norman tradition after the Conquest. The organization of tradition reflects the need to give an intellectual definition to a socio-geographic reality. The hold of the past is not only legal and cultural. It is also spatial. It is expressed in land and people, who are geographically placed, and may think they are divinely ordained, to mirror a particular tradition. Churches monumentalize these relations in medieval Europe, as do temple sites in Southeast Asia,[10] while pilgrimages ritualize relations between the centers and peripheries of religious experience.[11]

This outline of the typical features of traditions could be extended. But a mere enumeration does not tell us how tradition actually brings about change. This issue demands a different approach.

Before turning to this, one final caveat. If we are to come to grips with how tradition works, we must not only distance ourselves from the ideological positions that favor tradition or modernity. It is also necessary to abandon the naïve dichotomy "traditional/modern."[12] For here the traditional does not derive its sense from empirical or historical inquiry. The meaning arises from the rhetorical necessity of finding an opposite to "the modern." This is definition by default.

Now, there is something in societal change that corresponds roughly to the traditional and the modern, even if we speak of it in other terms. But the meaning of the pair cannot be firmly grounded until various types of traditions are themselves sorted out. Traditions are not all the same, and they do not react similarly in the face of change. Nor do societies change all at once: most are not traditional or modern but rather some combination of the two, as Levy, Geertz, and others illustrate.[13] Tradition and modernity are not mutually exclusive; they are mutually interdependent. If we date a society's change from the point at which the dichotomy traditional/modern is articulated, we are not really establishing very much. For we have not explained how the society got where it is, or why.

All medieval society was traditional in some sense. However, at various periods, it is possible to distinguish between what I would call *traditional* and *traditionalistic* action. Traditional action is substantive. It consists of the habitual pursuit of inherited forms of conduct, which are taken to be society's norm. Traditionalistic action, by contrast, is the self-conscious affirmation of traditional norms. It is the establishment of such norms as articulated models for current and future behavior. These guidelines imperfectly reflect the past, since at any given time individuals are only in contact with a part of their cultural heritage. Indeed, one of the features of traditionalistic action is that norms are consciously selected from the fund of traditional knowledge in order to serve present needs.

One does not have to look hard for examples of traditionalistic activity in medieval culture. They appear regularly in every "reform" or "renaissance" between later antiquity and the fifteenth century. They are particularly visible during the critical reassessment of the Christian heritage that took place during the eleventh and twelfth centuries. Wherever we look, we find a return to past models. Between 1057 and 1075 the Milanese Patarenes, invoking ancient precedents, battled against the entrenched rights of married priests. During the same century, traditionalism took a more intellectual form in the ecclesiological thought of Peter Damian and Gregory VII. Toward 1100, another variant is found in the wandering preachers of the northwest, such as Robert of Arbrissel, Bernard of Tiron, Vitalis of Savigny, and Norbert of Xanten. Their message was a literal imitation of the life of Christ as related in the gospels, while, in a different setting, Peter the Hermit preached an apocalyptic return to the age of the apostles once the Holy Land was in Christian hands. A generation later, Henry the Monk and Peter of Bruis, two preachers disappointed at the lack of rigor in the Gregorian reforms, taught that Christianity should shed the accretions it had acquired since New Testament times. Even anti-Semitism and dualism, two other popular religious tendencies in the period, had traditionalizing elements. Anti-Semitism had political roots, but anti-Jewish tracts invariably placed the central Jewish crime, the murder of Christ, in the distant past. The dualist contrasted a primitive state of affairs, a world of pure spirit, with the contamination of a material civilization that had grown up over time. There were many other versions of the traditionalizing thesis. Looking forward, one can see it diversely interpreted in the idea of *imitatio* in Peter Waldo and St. Francis.

At this point, an obvious question comes to mind. If all this is tradition, where is modernity?

The answer lies in looking more closely at what is happening. What I am describing is a widening gap between two sorts of activity, the traditional and the traditionalistic. This sometimes involves a dissociation between the practical and the theoretical—that is, between habitual activity that merely continues past practices without reflecting on them and self-conscious innovation based on the recovery of an allegedly authentic tradition. Thus Gregory VII is fond of distinguishing between "custom" and "truth." But there may also be a separation of the substantive and the formal, as, for instance, when canonists and churchmen joined forces in the thirteenth century to create an ecclesiastical bureaucracy in which great weight was placed on "rational" decision-making.

However we label these changes, their essence lies in ratiocination applied to tradition. The past is thought about, codified, and, as an abstraction, made a guide for action. The models may be simple, and rest on nothing more than a reaffirmation of the rule of St. Benedict; or they may be full-scale utopian schemes like those of Joachim of Floris. Viewed in the light of their common features, they constitute one of the period's strongest endogenous forces for change. For as the distance widened between the contrasting notions of tradition, the acceptance of the past and the rethinking of the past parted ways. There were equally valid, but incompatible, interpretations of what tradition meant. Traditionalistic action became a statement of past norms of conduct, not as they were, but as they were thought to be. And this restatement was considered by reformers to be more correct, truthful, and consistent than the welter of inherited customs that had been handed down from one generation to the next. The final stage of this evolution was the labeling of the two types of tradition in ways that brought about the contrast. One remained known as tradition. The other emerged as modernity.

Tradition is said to be created by the consciousness of modernity, much in the way that oral culture is set in relief by writing. But in the Middle Ages, modernity was more often than not the creation of tradition. For if the forces for interpreting stability and change came chiefly from within tradition, modernity is meaningful only as an aspect of traditionalistic behavior. Modernity, in this sense, occurs when the distance between the traditional and the traditionalistic is so great that the models can no longer be reconciled within individuals' minds. Practice now seems to dictate theory that the rationalized models supersede, and theory implies practices out of harmony with traditional norms. The great religious controversies of the eleventh and twelfth centuries—the debate over the Gregorian reforms, the rise and decline of monasticism, the tensions over investiture, and the growth of heresy and dissent— were all movements that involved differing perceptions of the past. As they moved from spontaneous to routinized types of behavior, forms of traditionalistic action even created new traditions in their wake.

True, modernity did not always emerge from tradition. Individuals occasionally saw themselves as breaking cleanly with what had always been thought and done. It is possible to read the initial chapters of Abelard's story in this way, as well as that of Héloïse, and, in a more psychological sense, of Hildegard of Bingen. In the thirteenth century, spiritual Franciscans like Peter John Olivi believed that the apostolic life could only be achieved through a decisive break with the historically evolving institutions of the church. There are other examples of discontinuity. One thinks of the growing merchant class in the towns, who lived in an ethical halfway house between salvation and profitability; of Jewish bankers and physicians, who had no vital interest in the perpetuation of Christian tradition; or of women in general, whom the traditions of the Church had so completely isolated that they could only achieve meaningful participation in religion through a symbolic inversion of its accepted procedures. Such individuals and groups are modern in a new sense. They think of themselves as belonging to an age whose internal coherence is more important than its links with the past; an age that is confident of its bearings and intellectual direction in contrast to the legacy of the southern Mediterranean world; and an age ready to complain of the lack of recognition of its achievements in the name of blind adherence to tradition. Just as the economy of northwestern Europe was enjoying its first surplus, so its thinkers were discovering new meanings for leisure. They were less embarrassed than they had been in the past at their society's *novitas*.

Yet, however we single out the poor, the marginal, the sexually disfavored, and the period's new men, it remains an inescapable reality of medieval life that none of these groups initiated major social or cultural changes before the thirteenth century. These all arose from within the mainstream, where modernity had different associations. Modernity did not come to a "traditional" society from the outside, like British government to Mughal India. It came from medieval society itself. The first sense of *modernus* in medieval Latin was that of a temporal distinctiveness from the age of the early Christians, either within the patristic age itself or in the writings of ninth-century reformers. As time went on, *moderni* emerged in the various medieval disciplines, such as logic and theology, in which there was a clear contrast between older and more recent practices. In the twelfth century, when *modernitas* first emerges as an idea capable of characterizing an age, its proponents are still looking backwards.[14] In the *Anticlaudianus,* Alan of Lille's *novus homo* is both a new and a renewed man.[15]

It is important not to be deceived by the period's false modernities. Modernity may be a definitive break with the past; but it may be nothing more than the reassertion of a neglected aspect of tradition. And at times it may be both. The two sides in the eucharistic debate between the ninth and the twelfth centuries both appealed to tradition. But both were modernist: no such debate took place among the ancients, and its scholastic solution would have been inconceivable in the patristic age. Again, modernity can masquerade as tradition. The codification of feudal and customary law in Europe from the twelfth century on created a realm of traditional practices, just as colonial administrators in nineteenth-century West Africa defined for the natives what was meant by "traditional law." However, by the late thirteenth century, "custom" reveals a new dynamism, often superseding the archaism of inherited written statutes.

Above all, one must not be taken in by the false modernity of literacy itself. Stage-theorists of culture are still fond of positing an oral, traditional past superseded by a period of writing, modernity, and openness to the present. Even Bakhtin, whose notion of dialogism has provided so much stimulus to literary analysis, fell into the trap of contrasting the epic and novelistic worlds as successive stages of cultural development. "The epic," he says, "is walled off absolutely from all subsequent times, and above all from those times in which the singer and his listeners are located," while "the novel, by contrast, is determined by experience, knowledge, and practice (the future)."[16] So defined, orality, epic discourse, and tradition are tautologies. But the novel, which Bakhtin saw emerging in Hellenism and later in Rabelais, also reworks tradition in subtle ways. There is not one tradition and one modernity, but rather different uses of tradition adapted to linguistic and social circumstances, in which the creation of the "epic past" is an indissoluble part of the creation of the discourse of modernity.

In a world of self-conscious reflection on the past, both tradition and modernity are discourses; and, as such, they may be thought of both as realities and as forms of social disguise. They need no longer be what on the surface they seem to be. Let me give one example. No figure in the twelfth century embodies the force of tradition as does St. Bernard. He is charismatic, authoritative, and the master of the century's major means of communication, the sermon. The essence of his message is monastic reform through a revival of the Benedictine tradition; and that is one genuine element in his discourse. But, as we look more closely at the saint, we see other interests, such as that of the rural aristocrat suspicious of the town and the nascent university milieu. More generally, we see the older agrarian system of great estates threatened by markets, cash crops, work contracts, entrepreneurs, and monetary exchange. These are among the subtexts in Bernard's discourse of tradition. Traditionality here is both a force for reformist change and a hegemony of the past, a form of historic nostalgia for an age that is passing away. Just as Bakhtin created a traditional past for the epic, so Bernard synthesized a heroic past for Eastern ascetic monasticism.

The example of Bernard raises another issue. This concerns the carriers of traditionalistic action. Viewed from the perspective of the twelfth century, it is not intellectuals but institutions that matter. This is one of the meanings of Bernard's victory over Abelard, which he won not as an individual alone but also as the representative of an institutional renewal. However, this was a battle, not the war. As one moves forward in time, the role of ideas grows.

There is no evidence that Bernard's monks knew, or cared, about the literary debate between a Cluniac and a Cistercian.[17] But it is doubtful whether anyone a century later joined the spiritual Franciscans without a grasp, however rudimentary, of the issues surrounding apostolic poverty. Tradition and modernity had by this time become both institutional and intellectual issues. Looking forward to the fourteenth century, we see another sort of shift. It is no longer religious groups that carry the debate. This now takes place chiefly in literature and art, whose vehicle is style. For reflections of modernity, we turn to Dante, Chaucer, and Petrarch. Clearly we must not only investigate the fact of modernity. We should also ask why we witness a transfer from institutions to ideas, literature, and art, and, if that is so, what it means. One thing it seems to mean is that revolutions can be started through forms of expression alone.

But there is also something to be learned about our attitude toward modernization. In general, we have given insufficient weight in European history to internal factors produced by reactions to tradition. We have thereby foreshortened our perspective on change itself. Among phenomena of long duration, traditionalistic action plays a significant role. True, there are disruptions: one thinks of technology, the Crusades, the Arab menace, and the shattering effects of wars, plagues, and famines. Science and economics, too, argue for discontinuities. But the most important long-term forces grow from within Europe's own social and cultural conventions. One of the tasks that awaits historical research is the sorting out of the long and short waves of tradition and modernity, and the setting up of a genuinely comparative model of change in Western and non-Western societies based on reactions to the inherited past.

The typical and atypical features of European development can thereby be thrown into relief more precisely than before. J. C. Heesterman argues that what characterizes tradition in Indian Hinduism is an "inner conflict of atemporal order and temporal shift" rather than "resilience and adaptiveness" in society.[18] But this circularity does not adequately describe how Christian tradition works in the Western Middle Ages. What is distinctive in its approach is its attempt to overcome the inner conflict of tradition, and this involves the birth of the notion of cultural progress as a way of transcending, and yet incorporating, the past. Modernity, as a by-product of tradition, emerges more positively in Christianity than it does in other scriptural religions, not only in comparison with Hinduism but also in contrast to its neighboring faiths in the West, Judaism and Islam. Christianity is not itself a modernizing faith—in essence no religion is—but during the Middle Ages it opened the door to what later became known as modernization. This can be viewed as an advance in civilization of a sort. But let us not be too quick to applaud. For it implied a transfer of conflict from symbolic to lived reality, and once that took place, a resolution could only be brought about in terms of human lives. That is one of the unfortunate lessons of the next five centuries of European history.

NOTES

CHAPTER ONE
History, Literature, Textuality

1. Cf. Hans Kellner, "Triangular Anxieties: The Present State of European Intellectual History," in *Modern European Intellectual History: Reappraisals and New Perspectives*, ed. Dominick La Capra and Steven L. Kaplan (Ithaca, N.Y., 1982), p. 114.

2. See ch. 7, pp. 140–58.

3. *Monumenta Germaniae Historica: Scriptores*, vol. 6, pp. 447–49.

4. *Anecdotes historiques, légendes et apologues tirés du recueil inédit d'Etienne de Bourbon, dominicain du XIIIᵉ siècle*, ed. A. Lecoy de la Marche (Paris, 1887), ch. 342, pp. 290–93.

5. See Malcolm Lambert, *Medieval Heresy: Popular Movements from Bogomil to Hus* (London, 1976), appendix C, pp. 352–55.

6. *Chronicon Laudunensis*, anno 1173, *MGH SS*, 6: 447, 34–40: "Is quadam die dominica cum declinasset ad turbam, quam ante ioculatorem viderat congregatam, ex verbis ipsius conpungtus fuit, et eum ad domum suam deducens, intente eum audire curavit. Fuit enim locus narracionis eius, qualiter beatus Alexis in domo patris sui beato fine quievit. Facto mane, civis memoratus ad scolas theologie consilium anime sue quesiturus properavit; et de multis modis eundi ad Deum edoctus, quesivit a magistro, que via aliis omnibus cercior esset atque perfeccior. Cui magister dominicam sentenciam proposuit: 'Si vis esse perfectus, vade et vende omnia que abes.'"

7. *Anecdotes historiques*, ch. 342, p. 291: "Quidam dives rebus in dicta urbe, dictus Waldensis, audiens evangelia, cum non esset multum litteratus, curiosus intelligere quid dicerent, fecit pactum cum dictis sacerdotibus [i.e., Bernardus Ydrus et Stephanus de Ansa], alteri ut

transferret ei in vulgari, alteri ut scriberet que ille dictaret, quod fece-
runt; similiter multos libros Biblie et auctoritates sanctorum multas
per titulos congregatas, quas sentencias appellabant. Que cum dictus
civis sepe legeret et cordetenus firmaret, proposuit servare perfectio-
nem evangelicam ut apostoli servaverant."
8. *Vita S. Antonii*, ch. 2, *Patrologia Graeca*, vol. 26, col. 841C.
9. *Anecdotes historiques*, ch. 342, pp. 292–92.
10. Lambert, *Medieval Heresy*, p. 68.

CHAPTER TWO
Medieval Literacy, Linguistic Theory, and Social Organization

1. Boethius, *Commentarii in Librum Aristotelis Peri ermeneias*, ed. C.
Meiser, vol. 1 (Leipzig, 1887), pp. 32–33. Elsewhere in this commentary
Boethius reveals a considerably more sophisticated notion of the sign.
For a lengthier discussion, see John Magee, *Boethius on Signification
and Mind* (Leiden, 1989).
2. For a similar illustration based on the metaphor of coinage, yet
modified in Abelard's direction, see Ferdinand de Saussure, *Cours de
linguistique générale*, ed. T. de Mauro (Paris, 1980), pp. 159–60, 164. For
a discussion of the widespread literary usage in the later Middle Ages,
see R. A. Shoaf, *Dante, Chaucer, and the Currency of the World: Money,
Images and Reference in Late Medieval Poetry* (Norman, Okla., 1983).
The issues are approached from another angle in Joel Kaye, "The
Impact of Money on the Development of Fourteenth-Century
Thought," *Journal of Medieval History* 14 (1988): 251–70.
3. For a useful review of these distinctions, applicable alike to linguistics
and anthropology, see Stephen A. Tyler, *The Said and the Unsaid:
Mind, Meaning, and Culture* (New York, 1978), pp. 3–19.
4. Ibid., p. 5.
5. For a review of the issues, see Jean Jolivet, *Arts du langage et théologie
chez Abélard* (Paris, 1969), pp. 13–115.
6. Cf. L. M. de Rijk, "The Semantical Impact of Abailard's Solution of
the Problem of Universals," in *Petrus Abaelardus, 1079–1142: Person,
Werk und Wirkung*, ed. R. Thomas et al. (Trier, 1980), p. 139.
7. Clifford Geertz, "Deep Play: Notes on the Balinese Cockfight," in *The
Interpretation of Cultures* (New York, 1973), p. 449.
8. Jacques Derrida, *De la grammatologie* (Paris, 1967), pp. 149–202. On

the medieval implications of this debate, see R. Howard Bloch, *Etymologies and Genealogies: A Literary Anthropology of the French Middle Ages* (Chicago, 1983), pp. 1-29.

9. Erving Goffman, *The Presentation of Self in Everyday Life* (New York, 1959); id., *Relations in Public* (New York, 1971).

10. Paul Ricoeur, *Freud and Philosophy: An Essay in Interpretation*, trans. D. Savage (New Haven, 1970), pp. 26-27.

11. M. Meggitt, "Uses of Literacy in New Guinea and Melanesia," in *Literacy in Traditional Societies*, ed. Jack Goody (Cambridge, 1968), p. 302.

12. Ambrogio Calepino, *Dictionarii Octolinguis* (Lyon, 1663), p. 703, s.v. *textum*.

13. Charles du Fresne du Cange et al. *Glossarium ad Scriptores Mediae et Infimae Latinitatis*, vol. 6 (Paris, 1736), p. 1113, s.v. *textus*.

14. Cicero *De Natura Deorum* 2.150.

15. Alexander Souter, *A Glossary of Later Latin to 600 A.D.* (Oxford, 1949), s.v. *texta*.

16. Jack Goody, "Restricted Literacy in Northern Ghana," in *Literacy in Traditional Societies*, p. 227.

17. Gottlob Frege, "On Sense and Reference," in *Translations from the Philosophical Writings of Gottlob Frege*, ed. Peter Geach and Max Black (Oxford, 1970), pp. 57-58.

18. Peter Abelard, *Sic et Non, prologus*, in *Patrologia Latina*, vol. 178, cols. 1339A-1343D.

19. Boethius, *Commentarii* 23.16-18.

20. Cf. Paul Ricoeur, "The hermeneutical Function of Distanciation," in *Hermeneutics and the Human Sciences: Essays on Language, Action, and Interpretation*, ed. and trans. J. B. Thompson (Cambridge and Paris, 1981), p. 140.

21. Bernard Guenée, "Temps de l'histoire et temps de la mémoire au moyen âge," in *Annuaire-Bulletin de la Société de l'histoire de France*, *Années 1976-77* (Paris, 1978), p. 29.

22. K. F. Werner, "Untersuchungen zur Frühzeit des französischen Fürstentums (9.-10. Jahrhundert), *Die Welt als Geschichte* 18 (1958): 256-89; 19 (1959): 146-93; 20 (1960): 87-119.

23. Georges Duby, "Structures de parenté et noblesse dans la France du Nord aux XIe et XIIe siècles," in *Hommes et structures du moyen âge* (Paris, 1973), pp. 282-83.

24. Ibid., p. 283. For an excellent overview of the issues, see Gabrielle M.

Spiegel, "Genealogy: Form and Function in Medieval Historical Narrative," *History and Theory* 22 (1983): 43–53.

25. Paul Alphandéry, *La chrétienté et l'idée de croisade*, vol. 1, *Les premières croisades*, ed. A. Dupront (Paris, 1954), p. 9.

26. Ludwig Wittgenstein, *The Blue and Brown Books* (Oxford, 1958), p. 143.

CHAPTER THREE
Romantic Attitudes and Academic Medievalism

1. George Duby, *Des sociétés médiévales: Leçon inaugurale au Collège de France* (Paris, 1971), recalling Lucien Febvre and Marc Bloch (p. 8).

2. For an interpretation of *mentalité* in sociohistorical terms, see Duby, "Histoire des mentaliés," in *Encyclopédie de la Pléiade: L'histoire et ses méthodes*, ed. C. Samaran (Paris, 1961), pp. 937–66. Another perspective is offered by Jacques Le Goff, "Les mentalités: Une histoire ambiguë," in *Faire l'histoire*, vol. 3, ed. J. Le Goff and P. Nora (Paris, 1974), pp. 76–94.

3. Keith Thomas, "History and Anthropology," *Past and Present* 24 (1963): 3.

4. Compare the resistance to theory in the reviews of Kantorowicz's *The King's Two Bodies: A Study in Mediaeval Political Theology* (Princeton, 1957), by R. W. Southern, *Journal of Ecclesiastical History* 10 (1959): 104–8, and Beryl Smalley, *Past and Present* 20 (1961): 30–35, with the warmer reception of Walter Ullmann, *Mitteilungen des Oesterreichische Geschichtsforschung* 66 (1958): 364–69. Kantorowicz is one of a handful of medievalists of his generation whose methods influenced other fields; see S. J. Tambiah, *World Conqueror and World Renouncer: A Study of Buddhism and Polity in Thailand against a Historical Background* (Cambridge, 1976), p. 7.

5. For example, Hans Robert Jauss, "Littérature médiévale et théorie des genres," *Poétique* 1 (1970): 79–101. Medieval titles are found in the comprehensive bibliography of Georges Gurvitch, *Les cadres sociaux de la connaissance* (Paris, 1966), pp. 258–310. What used to be called "sociology" in medieval literary studies is now more appropriately called "anthropology"; see Bloch, *Etymologies and Genealogies*, pp. 1–29. For a French example, using the methods of folklore and anthropology, see J.-C. Schmitt, *Le saint lévrier: Guinefort, guérisseur d'enfants depuis de XIIIᵉ siècle* (Paris, 1979); on the method, from a historical standpoint,

see Jacques Le Goff, *Pour un autre moyen âge: Temps, travail et culture en Occident: 18 essais* (Paris, 1977), parts 3 and 4.

6. Erich Auerbach, *Literatursprache und Publikum in der lateinischen Spätantike und im Mittelalter* (Bern, 1958). A bibliography of Auerbach's writings is found in the English translation, *Literary Language and Its Public in Late Latin Antiquity and in the Middle Ages*, trans. Ralph Manheim (London, 1965), and in his *Gesammelte Aufsätze zur romanischen Philologie* (Bern, 1967), pp. 365–69.

7. Auerbach, *Literatursprache und Publikum*, pp. 9–10.

8. Erich Auerbach, *Mimesis: Dargestellte Wirklichkeit in der abendländischen Literatur*, 3d. ed. (Bern and Munich, 1964), p. 512; trans. W. R. Trask, *Mimesis: The Representation of Reality in Western Literature* (New York, 1953), pp. 486–87. For Auerbach's comments on the book, see "Epilegomena zu Mimesis," *Romanische Forschungen* 65 (1954): 1–18; and, on the broader context of the issues, Karl F. Morrison, *The Mimetic Tradition of Reform in the West* (Princeton, 1982); on Auerbach, pp. 404–14. Auerbach's outlook is also the subject of Luiz Costa-Lima, "Erich Auerbach: History and Metahistory," *New Literary History* 19 (1988): 467–99.

9. Had Carlo Antoni's engaging *Dallo storicismo alla soziologia*, 2d ed. (Florence, 1951), not been finished before World War II, a chapter might have been added on Auerbach and the decline of Romance philology. In the introduction to his translation, *From History to Sociology: The Transition in German Historical Thinking* (Detroit, 1959), xx–xxi, Hayden White provides a useful summary of aesthetic historicist tendencies. See as well Charles Breslin, "Philosophy or Philology: Auerbach and Aesthetic Historicism," *Journal of the History of Ideas* 22 (1961): 369–81. For a detailed review of the decline of historicism, see Georg G. Iggers, *The German Conception of History: The National Tradition in Historical Thought from Herder to the Present* (Middletown, Conn. 1968), pp. 125–268.

10. Auerbach, "Vico and Aesthetic Historism" (an address), in *Gesammelte Aufsätze*, pp. 266–74; cf. "Philologie der Weltliteratur," ibid., pp. 310–10, and the introduction to *Literatursprache und Publikum*.

11. Spitzer outlines his intellectual development in the address "Linguistics and Literary History," in *Linguistics and Literary History: Essays in Stylistics* (New York, 1962), pp. 1–39, and acknowledges a debt to Auerbach in "The Epic Style of the Pilgrim Aetheria," rpt. in *Romanische*

Literaturstudien, 1936–1956 (Tübingen, 1959), p. 905. For Auerbach's debt to Spitzer, see *Mimesis*, trans. W. Trask, p. 363; and, on their personal relations, Morrison, *Mimetic Tradition of Reform*, pp. 399–414.

12. Auerbach, *Literary Language*, p. 19.
13. Auerbach, *Mimesis*, p. 7: *ausgeformen:* p. 10: *ausgeformt;* p. 29: *ausformende Beschreibung*, etc.
14. Heinrich Wölfflin, *Kunstgeschichtliche Grundbegriffe*, 6th ed. (Basel, 1923), appears to anticipate Auerbach's preoccupation with the formal aspects of representation in part 2 of his introduction, where he speaks of the "Art der Auffassung, die den darstellenden Künsten in den Verschiedenen Jahrhunderten zugrunde liegt" as a division into "Darstellungsformen" (p. 14). In other ways, Auerbach and Wölfflin differ, especially on the notion of empathy and in the latter's neo-Kantianism; see the exposition of Wölfflin's ideas by Michael Podro, *The Critical Historians of Art* (New Haven, 1982), pp. 98–116.
15. Auerbach, *Mimesis*, p. 8.
16. Ibid. Auerbach treats St. Francis in a similar perspective: "Über das Persönliche in der Wirkung des heiligen Franz von Assisi," and "Franz von Assisi in der *Komödie*," reprinted in *Gesammelte Aufsätze*, pp. 33–42, 43–54. Auerbach's view of the individuality of St. Francis, together with his deemphasizing of the Renaissance as a decisive break in style, places him in the tradition of Renan and of Henry Thode's influential, but inaccurate, *Franz von Assisi und die Anfänge der Kunst der Renaissance in Italien* (Berlin, 1885); see Wallace K. Ferguson, *The Renaissance in Historical Thought: Five Centuries of Interpretation* (Cambridge, Mass., 1948), pp. 298–302. The idea that naturalism occurred in medieval thought and artistic expression before it appeared in Renaissance painting is also maintained by W. Goetz, "Die Entwicklung des Wirklichkeitssinnes vom 12. zum 14. Jahrhundert," *Archiv für Kulturgeschichte* 27 (1937): 33–73. One of the chief twelfth-century exponents was Bernardus Silvestris; see my *Myth and Science in the Twelfth Century: A Study of Bernard Silvester* (Princeton, 1972), pp. 63–87, 97–118, 227–73.
17. Auerbach, *Mimesis*, trans. Trask, p. 33.
18. Ibid., p. 46.
19. Augustine, *Confessions* 6.8.
20. Erich Auerbach, *Dante als Dichter der irdischen Welt* (Berlin and Leipzig, 1929). However, this was not the weakness that most forcefully

struck Auerbach's critics, who gave his innovative book almost universally poor reviews. An exception was Etienne Gilson, who noted the book's value, "Le moyen âge et le naturalisme antique," *Archives d'histoire doctrinale et littéraire du moyen âge* 7 (1932): 490.

21. *Mimesis*, trans. Trask, p. 490.

22. Auerbach is using A. von Harnack's term *Pendelausschlag* as a metaphor for dialectical movement; *Mimesis*, p. 36.

23. *Mimesis*, trans. Trask, pp. 36-37.

24. See Peter Dronke, *Classical Review*, n.s., 16 (1966): 362-63.

25. Erich Auerbach, *Vier Untersuchungen zur Geschichte der französischen Bildung* (Bern, 1951), pp. 12-50; trans. Ralph Manheim, *Scenes from the Drama of European Literature: Six Essays by Erich Auerbach* (New York, 1959), pp. 133-79.

26. Auerbach, *Literary Language*, pp. 237-38.

27. Conversely, one may ask whether semiotics has not resurrected a good deal of medieval literary theory. R. Jakobson, *Essais de linguistique générale* (Paris, 1963), p. 162, cites the classical definition of metaphor in its medieval Latin form, *aliquid stat pro aliquo*. Both Barthes and Foucault maintained that structuralism was anticipated by rhetoric, a view that neatly recapitulates the transition from Augustinian to Thomistic aesthetics. In early papers, both Julia Kristeva and Jacques Derrida refer to the medieval roots of the discipline; see their respective essays, "Le lieu sémiotique" and "Sémiologie et grammatologie," in *Essays in Semiotics*, ed. J. Kristeva (Paris, 1971), pp. 1, 13. From Augustine onwards, it was normal for philosophers to think of language as a system of signs; see Marcia Colish, *The Mirror of Language: A Study in the Medieval Theory of Language* (New Haven, 1968). There are suggestive remarks in Umberto Eco, *Il problema estetico in Tommaso d'Aquino* (Milan, 1970), pp. 259-63, and an application to medieval literature and art in S. G. Nichols, Jr., *Romanesque Signs: Early Medieval Narrative and Iconography* (New Haven, 1983).

28. N. Edelman, *Attitudes of Seventeenth-Century France toward the Middle Ages* (New York, 1946), pp. 2-3. Cf. A. Pauphilet, "Le mythe du moyen âge," in *Le legs du moyen âge: Etudes de littérature médiévale* (Melun, 1950), pp. 22-63.

29. See, on the Bollandist and Maurist collections, David Knowles, *Great Historical Enterprises: Problems in Monastic History* (London, 1963), pp. 1-62.

30. Students of postmedieval periods often overlook the fact that *moder-*

nus and *modernitas* were first used to indicate a shift in historical outlook and a concern with the internal, horizontal bonds within periods of time in the twelfth century; see ch. 8.

31. Douglas Bush, *English Literature in the Earlier Seventeenth Century* (Oxford, 1945), p. 1. The question is reviewed by Paolo Rossi, *Francesco Bacone: Dalla magia alla scienza* (Bari, 1957; English trans., Chicago and London, 1968).

32. See the excellent study of Lionel Gossman, *Medievalism and the Ideologies of the Enlightenment: The World and Work of La Curne de Sainte-Palaye* (Baltimore, 1968).

33. Johann Gottfried Herder, *Auch eine Philosophie der Geschichte zur Bildung der Menschheit* (Riga, 1774) quoted in *J. G. Herder on Social and Political Culture*, ed. F. M. Barnard (Cambridge, 1969), p. 184.

34. Ibid., pp. 191-92.

35. Friedrich Meinecke, *Historism: The Rise of a New Historical Outlook* (London, 1972), p. 337. A similar position was arrived at independently by Ernst Cassirer, *The Problem of Knowledge: Philosophy, Science and History since Hegel* (New Haven, 1950), p. 222.

36. Cf. S. Avineri, *The Social and Political Thought of Karl Marx* (Cambridge, 1969), p. 158. The idea was carried over into medieval research; see Marc Bloch, *La société féodale*, vol. 1, *La formation des liens de dépendence* (Paris, 1939), pp. 1-8.

37. Meinecke, *Historism*, p. 339, who adds: "Herder may well have been more successful in his attempted universal history at bringing out the value of the Middle Ages as a stage of development than in its own intrinsic qualities."

38. For a corrective to the widely held English and American view that medieval Latin studies were invented by the Germans, see the works of Knowles (cited n. 29 above) and Gossman (n. 32 above), in the latter esp. pp. 197-215, 349-58. Karl Strecker's useful *Introduction to Medieval Latin* (rpt. Zürich, 1965), made an unwitting contribution to this view by allowing the history of the subject as presented to coincide with the beginnings of the German national tradition in the ninth century. English, Italian, and French studies long preceded those of the distinguished Ludwig Traube; and there is no break in the continuity of classical and medieval Latin in the ninth century that would justify so dramatic a neglect of earlier writing.

39. J. Bédier, "La tradition manuscrite du Lai de L'Ombre: Réflexions sur

l'art d'éditer les anciens textes," *Romania* 54 (1928): 161–96, 321–56. See also A. Castellani, *Bédier avait-il raison? La méthode de Lachmann dans les éditions de textes du moyen âge* (Fribourg, 1957). Recent opinion has swung away from the notion of a single "correct" version to which others are reduced. Influential in this regard is Paul Zumthor's notion of *mouvance,* which privileges the oral element; see his *Essai de poétique médiévale* (Paris, 1972), p. 74. For a recent example, see *The Songs of Jaufré Rudel,* ed. Rupert T. Pickens (Toronto, 1978). For an example of the shift back to the manuscript, see the forthcoming facsimile edition of Bibliothèque Nationale, Paris, MS fr. 146 by E. Roesner, Nancy Regalado, and F. Avril. For a brief, but outstanding, review of the issues, see Bernard Cerquiglini, *Eloge de la variante: Histoire critique de la philologie* (Paris, 1989).

40. A weak reflection of both traditions may be found in Paul Maas, *Textual Criticism* (Oxford, 1958), pp. 10–11. In discussing *examinatio,* Maas first establishes the Enlightenment principle that authority must yield to correctness. Then, quoting Wilamowitz, he notes that in cases of doubt the editor must follow his intuitive grasp of style and his organic understanding of the period.

41. See Otto Hintze, *Soziologie und Geschichte,* ed. G. Ostreich (Göttingen, 1964).

42. The best guide to the literature is Iordan-Orr, *An Introduction to Romance Linguistics: Its Schools and Scholars, Revised with a Supplement Thirty Years On by R. Posner* (Oxford, 1970), pp. 20–24 and passim.

43. For example, Vladimir Propp, *Morphology of the Folktale* (1928); trans. Laurence Scott, 2d ed. (Austin, 1968). A useful account of the Russian formalists is Frederic Jameson, *The Prison-House of Language: A Critical Account of Structuralism and Russian Formalism* (Princeton, 1972), pp. 43–98. The often-neglected contribution of Czech authors is discussed by F. W. Galan, *Historic Structures: The Prague School Project, 1928–1946* (Austin, 1985).

44. Eric Hobsbawm, *Industry and Empire* (Harmondsworth, 1969), p. 91.

CHAPTER FOUR

Literary Discourse and the Social Historian

1. Cf. Hayden White, "Interpretation in History," in *Tropics of Discourse: Essays in Cultural Criticism* (Baltimore, 1978), pp. 51–80. Cf. Nancy

Partner, "Making Up Lost Time: Writing on the Writing of History,"
Speculum 61 (1986): 90–117.

2. See Lawrence Stone, "The Revival of Narrative: Reflections on a New
Old History," in *The Past and the Present* (Boston, 1981), pp. 74–96. On
the uniting of narrative and the aims of social history, see Natalie
Zemon Davis, *Fiction in the Archives: Pardon Tales and Their Tellers in
Sixteenth-Century France* (Stanford, 1987).

3. Hans Liebeschütz, *Ranke*, Historical Association Publications G.3
(London, 1954), p. 3.

4. See, for example, Michel de Certeau, *The Practice of Everyday Life* (Berkeley and Los Angeles, 1984).

5. For a recent review of the issues, see the essays of James Clifford, *The
Predicament of Culture: Twentieth-Century Ethnography, Literature,
and Art* (Cambridge, Mass., 1988).

6. Cf. Robert Darnton, *The Great Cat Massacre and Other Episodes in
French Cultural History* (New York, 1985), pp. 257–63.

7. Claude Lévi-Strauss, *La pensée sauvage* (1962), anonymously trans. as
The Savage Mind (Chicago, 1966), pp. 245–69.

8. Marc Bloch, "Les formes de la rupture de l'hommage dans l'ancien
droit féodal," in *Mélanges historiques*, vol. 1 (Paris, 1963), pp. 189–206.

9. For an enduring study of these issues, see Georges Duby, *La société aux
XIe et XIIe siècles dans la région mâconnaise*, 2d ed. (Paris, 1971).

10. Max Weber, *Wirtschaft und Gesellschaft: Grundriss der verstehenden
Soziologie*, ed. J. Winckelmann, 5th ed. (Tübingen, 1972), p. 1.

11. For a further discussion of these issues, see ch. 6.

12. Weber has been most systematically criticized with respect to his
vagueness on subjective meaning by Alfred Schutz, *The Phenomenology of the Social World*, trans. G. Walsh and F. Lehnert (Evanston, Ill.,
1967), pp. 3–44.

13. Ernst Cassirer, *The Philosophy of Symbolic Forms*, vol. 3 of *The Phenomenology of Knowledge*, trans. Ralph Manheim (New Haven, 1957), p.
262.

14. Victor Turner, *Dramas, Fields, and Metaphors: Symbolic Action in
Human Society* (Ithaca, N.Y., 1974), p. 23.

15. Ibid., p. 13.

16. Mary Douglas, *Purity and Danger: An Analysis of Concepts of Pollution and Taboo* (London, 1966), p. 162. Cf. Godfrey Lienhardt, *Divinity and Experience: The Religion of the Dinka* (Oxford, 1961), p. 291.

17. Two studies that focus on ritual in the context of typologies are: Natalie Zemon Davis, "The Reason of Misrule: Youth Groups and Charivaris in Sixteenth-Century France," *Past and Present* 50 (1971): 41-75, and Jacques Le Goff and Emmanuel Le Roy Ladurie "Mélusine maternelle et défricheuse," *Annales: Economies, sociétés, civilisations* 26 (1971): 587-622. There are a growing number of studies that use interpretive anthropology as a basis for understanding medieval culture. Examples include Peter Brown, "Society and the Supernatural: A Medieval Change," in *Society and the Holy in Late Antiquity* (Berkeley and Los Angeles, 1982), pp. 302-32; Rebecca V. Colman, "Reason and Unreason in Early Medieval Law," *Journal of Interdisciplinary History* 4 (1974): 571-91; Georges Duby, "Les «jeunes» dans la société aristocratique dans la France du Nord-Ouest au XIIe siècle," in *Hommes et structures du moyen âge* (Paris, 1973), pp. 213-25; Patrick Geary, "Sacred Commodities: The Circulation of Medieval Relics," in *The Social Life of Things: Commodities in Cross-Cultural Perspective*, ed. A. Appadurai (Cambridge, 1986), pp. 169-91; Jack Goody, *The Development of the Family and Marriage in Europe* (Cambridge, 1983); A. Y. Gurevitch, "Wealth and Gift-Bestowal among the Ancient Scandinavians," *Scandinavia* 7 (1968): 126-38; Diane Hughes, "Distinguishing Signs: Ear-Rings, Jews and Franciscan Rhetoric in the Italian Renaissance City," *Past and Present* 112 (1986): 3-59; Paul Hyams, "Trial by Ordeal: The Key to Proof in Early Common Law," in *On Laws and Customs of England: Essays in Honor of Samuel E. Thorne*, ed. M. S. Arnold et al. (Chapel Hill, 1982), pp. 90-126; Mervyn James, "Ritual Drama, and Social Body in the Late Medieval English Town," *Past and Present* 98 (1983): 3-29; William Ian Miller, "Choosing the Avenger: Some Aspects of the Bloodfeud in Medieval Iceland and England," *Law and History Review* 1 (1983): 161-204; Alexander C. Murray, *Germanic Kinship Structure: Studies in Law and Society in Antiquity and the Middle Ages* (Toronto, 1983); Stephen D. White, "'Pactem ... Legem Vincit et Amor Judicium': The Settlement of Disputes by Compromise in Eleventh-Century Western France," *American Journal of Legal History* 22 (1978): 281-309. For an overview by a historian, see Natalie Zemon Davis, "Anthropology and History in the 1980s: The Possibilities of the Past," *Journal of Interdisciplinary History* 12 (1981): 267-75, and, from a literary perspective, Bloch, *Etymologies and Genealogies*, pp. 1-29.

CHAPTER FIVE

Language and Culture: Saussure, Ricoeur, and Foucault

1. Hannah Arendt, *The Life of the Mind*, ed. Mary McCarthy (New York, 1978), 1: 19–20.
2. Hilary Putnam, *Reason, Truth, and History* (Cambridge, 1981), pp. xi, 1.
3. Ibid., p. 19.
4. I base the following on Saussure's own summary of his position, *Cours de linguistique générale* (1916), ed. Tullio de Mauro (Paris, 1981), pp. 31–32; translations are my own.
5. Ibid., p. 36.
6. Ibid., p. 43; cf. also p. vii.
7. Ibid., pp. 44–45.
8. Paul de Man, "Semiology and Rhetoric," in *Allegories of Reading* (New Haven, 1979), p. 6.
9. Compare Foucault, *L'ordre du discours* (Paris, 1971), pp. 7–10, where *discours* is conceived in an oral mode, with ibid., pp. 23ff. (*le commentaire*); pp. 28ff. (*l'auteur*); and pp. 31ff. (*l'organisation des disciplines*), all notions that involve writing.
10. See ch. 2, pp. 37–40.
11. Saussure, *Cours*, p. 45; cf. also p. 52.
12. Paul Ricoeur, *Interpretation Theory: Discourse and the Surplus of Meaning* (Fort Worth, Texas, 1976), pp. 9, 5.
13. Ibid., p. 9.
14. I am summarizing pp. 9–37 of ibid., with deliberate omissions.
15. Ibid., p. 12.
16. Ibid., p. 26, following Jakobson's "Linguistics and Poetics," in *Style in Language*, ed. T. A. Sebeok (Cambridge, Mass., 1960), pp. 350–77.
17. Ibid., p. 27.
18. Ibid., pp. 29–30.
19. Paul Ricoeur, "The Hermeneutical Function of Distanciation," in id., *Hermeneutics and the Human Sciences: Essays on Language, Action and Interpretation*, ed. and trans. John B. Thompson (Cambridge, 1981), pp. 131–44. For earlier statements of these ideas, see the bibliography in ibid. pp. vii–viii. Ricoeur subsequently tested these ideas against other philosophies of history; see his *Temps et récit* (Paris, 1983), published in English as *Time and Narrative*, 2 vols., trans. K. McLaughlin and D. Pellauer (Chicago, 1984).

20. Ricoeur, "Hermeneutical Function of Distanciation," p. 131.
21. Ibid., p. 132.
22. Ibid.
23. Ibid.
24. Ibid.
25. Ibid.
26. Ibid., p. 133.
27. Ibid., p. 134.
28. Ibid., p. 136.
29. Ibid., p. 142.
30. Ibid., p. 143.
31. Foucault, *L'ordre du discours*, pp. 10–23.
32. But see Hayden White, "Foucault's Discourse: The Historiography of Anti-Humanism," in *The Content of the Form: Narrative Discourse and Historical Representation* (Baltimore, 1987), pp. 104–41.

CHAPTER SIX
Max Weber, Western Rationality, and the Middle Ages

1. See *Dynamo and Virgin Reconsidered: Essays in the Dynamism of Western Culture* (Cambridge, Mass., 1968), chs. 1 and 2.
2. David C. Lindberg, ed., *Science in the Middle Ages* (Chicago, 1978), in which see, in particular, Lindberg's preface, pp. vii–xv, and my essay, "Science, Technology, and Economic Progress in the Early Middle Ages," pp. 1–51. A more recent statement is Nicholas H. Steneck, "The Relevance of the Middle Ages to the History of Science and Technology," in *Science and Technology in Medieval Society*, ed. Pamela O. Long, Annals of the New York Academy of Sciences, vol. 441 (New York, 1985), pp. 21–27.
3. For somewhat different perspectives, see Alexander Murray, *Reason and Society in the Middle Ages* (Oxford, 1978), part 3, and Nancy Siraisi, *Arts and Sciences at Padua: The 'Studium' of Padua before 1350* (Toronto, 1973).
4. See Kurt Vogel, "Fibonacci, Leonardo," *Dictionary of Scientific Biography*, 4: 604–13. Connections between mathematics and philosophy have been explored in a number of studies by John Murdoch; see, for instance, "*Mathesis in philosophiam scholasticam introducta*: The Rise and Development of the Application of Mathematics in Fourteenth-

Century Philosophy and Theology," in *Arts libéraux et philosophie au moyen âge: Actes du quatrième Congrès international de philosophie médiévale* (Montréal, 1969), pp. 215–64.

5. "Diskussionsrede zu E. Troeltschs Vortrag über 'Das stoisch-christliche Naturrecht,'" in Max Weber, *Gesammelte Aufsätze zur Soziologie und Sozialpolitik* (Tübingen, 1923), pp. 462–70.

6. For the dates of the various compositions in vol. 1 of Weber's *Gesammelte Aufsätze zur Religionssoziologie*, see D. Käsler, "Max-Weber-Bibliographie," *Kölner Zeitschrift für Soziologie und Sozialpsychologie* 27 (1975): 703–30.

7. The original criticism and replies are reprinted in *Max Weber: Die protestantische Ethik II. Kritiken und Anti-kritiken*, ed. J. Winckelmann, 2d ed. (Hamburg, 1972), pp. 1–345. The subsequent literature up to the time of its publication is covered in *Max Weber Bibliographie: Eine Dokumentation der Sekundärliteratur*, ed. G. Seyfarth and G. Schmidt (Stuttgart, 1977).

8. See A. Mitzman, *The Iron Cage: An Historical Interpretation of Max Weber* (New York, 1970), pp. 15–38.

9. In general, see W. Mommsen, *Max Weber und die deutsche Politik, 1890–1920*, 2d ed. (Tübingen, 1974).

10. See the much discussed essay of F. H. Tenbruck, "Das Werk Max Webers," *Kölner Zeitschrift für Soziologie und Sozialpsychologie* 27 (1975): 663–702; partial English trans., "The Problem of Thematic Unity in the Works of Max Weber," *British Journal of Sociology* 31 (1980): 313–51. Particularly important among responses is Wolfʒang Schluchter, *The Rise of Western Rationalism. Max Weber's Developmental History*, trans., with an introduction by Günther Roth (Berkeley and Los Angeles, 1981).

11. Max Weber, *The Protestant Ethic and the Spirit of Capitalism*, trans. T. Parsons (New York, 1930), p. 284 n. 119.

12. For a more extensive discussion, see ch. 8.

13. Edward Shils, *Tradition* (Chicago, 1981), p. 8.

14. Ferguson, *Renaissance in Historical Thought*, chs. 10 and 11. Weber's influence is understated in this classic study; see pp. 230, 232.

15. Keith Thomas, *Religion and the Decline of Magic: Studies in Popular Beliefs in Sixteenth- and Seventeenth-Century England* (Harmondsworth, 1973), pp. 27–57.

16. For a more extensive discussion of these issues, see my study *The Impli-*

cations of Literacy: Written Language and Models of Interpretation in the Eleventh and Twelfth Centuries (Princeton, 1983), esp. chs. 1, 2, and 3. In what follows, I draw on some of the examples from this study, without always reiterating that this is their source.

17. Schluchter, Rise of Western Rationalism, pp. 31-32. For a recent discussion, see Schluchter, "Religion, politische Herrschaft, Wirtschaft and bürgerliche Lebensführung," in Max Webers Sicht des okzidentalen Christentums: Interpretation und Kritik (Frankfurt, 1988), pp. 11-128.

18. See Reinhard Bendix, Max Weber: An Intellectual Portrait (Berkeley and Los Angeles, 1977); Günther Roth and Wolfgang Schluchter, Max Weber's Vision of History (Berkeley, 1979), esp. chs. 1, 3, and 5; Stephen Kalberg, "Max Weber's Types of Rationality: Cornerstones for the Analysis of Rationalization Processes in History," American Journal of Sociology 85 (1980): 1145-79; Donald N. Levine, "Rationality and Freedom: Weber and Beyond," Sociological Inquiry 51 (1981): 5-25. For further bibliography up to the time of their publication, see Kalberg and Levine, respectively pp. 1178-79 and pp. 23-25; earlier literature is also reviewed in Roth and Schluchter (1979), 13-14 nn. 7-8. For an attempt to revise Bendix's position, see Tenbruck, "Das Werk Max Webers" (cited in n. 10 above), pp. 663-702, and the sensible reply of Schluchter, Rise of Western Rationalism, pp. 3-5.

19. Cf. Schluchter, Rise of Western Rationalism, p. 12.

20. S. N. Eisenstadt, A Sociological Approach to Comparative Civilizations: The Development and Directions of a Research Program (Jerusalem, 1986), p. 44.

21. Max Weber, The Religion of China: Confucianism and Taoism, trans. and ed. Hans H. Gerth (Glencoe, Ill., 1951), p. 123 (= Gesammelte Aufsätze zur Religionssoziologie, vol. 1 [Tübingen, 1920-21], p. 412). Readers interested in the growth of literacy in China can now turn to the excellent study of Evelyn S. Rawski, Education and Popular Literacy in Ch'ing China (Ann Arbor, Mich., 1979).

22. Jürgen Habermas, The Theory of Communicative Action, vol. 1, Reason and the Rationalization of Society, trans. T. McCarthy (Boston, 1984) (= Theorie des Kommunikativen Handelns, vol. 1, Handlungsrationalität und gesellschaftliche Rationalisierung [Frankfurt, 1981]). For a broad reflection of the issues, see also Bryan R. Wilson, ed., Rationality (Oxford, 1974).

23. Max Weber, Economy and Society: An Outline of Interpretive Sociology,

ed. Günther Roth and Claus Wittich, vol. 1 (New York, 1968), p. 24.
24. Cf. C. W. Bynum, "Did the Twelfth Century Discover the Individual?" in *Jesus as Mother: Studies in the Spirituality of the High Middle Ages* (Berkeley and Los Angeles, 1982), p. 84. For an interesting review of the issues in literary perspective, see Gerald Bond, "Ovid's 'Heroides', Baudri of Bourgueil, and the Problem of Person," *Mediaevalia* 11 (1989), forthcoming.
25. Cf. Jeffrey C. Alexander, *Theoretical Logic in Sociology*, vol. 3, *The Classical Attempt at Theoretical Synthesis: Max Weber* (Berkeley and Los Angeles, 1983), p. 18.
26. Levine, "Rationality and Freedom," pp. 10–11.
27. Kalberg, "Max Weber's Types of Rationality," p. 1165.
28. For an outstanding study of these issues, see Michel Zink, *La subjectivité littéraire: Autour du siècle de saint Louis* (Paris, 1985).
29. Cf. Kalberg, "Max Weber's Types of Rationality," p. 1146 n. 2 and Tenbruck, "Thematic Unity in the Works of Max Weber" (cited in n. 10 above), p. 319, translator's note.
30. Hans Liebeschütz, "Max Weber's Historical Interpretation of Judaism," *Publications of the Leo Baeck Institute: Year Book* 9 (1964): 67.
31. See M.-D. Chenu's enduring essay, "La Nature et l'homme: La renaissance du XIIe siècle," in *La Théologie au douzième siècle* (Paris, 1957), pp. 19–51. There is now a large bibliography on this subject; for a recent reassessment of the achievements of twelfth-century culture, see *Renaissance and Renewal in the Twelfth Century*, ed. Robert L. Benson and Giles Constable, with Carol D. Lanham (Cambridge, Mass., 1982).
32. See S. N. Eisenstadt, "Max Webers antikes Judentum und der Charakter der jüdischen Zivilisation," in *Max Webers Studie über das antike Judentum*, ed. W. Schluchter (Frankfurt, 1981), pp. 134–84.
33. Tenbruck, "Thematic Unity in the Works of Max Weber," p. 320.
34. Jacob Neusner, *The Oral Torah: The Sacred Books of Judaism* (San Francisco, 1986), p. vii.
35. William A. Graham, "Qur'ān as Spoken Word: An Islamic Contribution to the Understanding of Scripture," in *Approaches to Islam in Religious Studies*, ed. Richard C. Martin (Tucson, 1985), p. 29.

CHAPTER SEVEN
Textual Communities:
Judaism, Christianity, and the Definitional Problem

1. Jack Goody, *The Domestication of the Savage Mind* (Cambridge, 1977), p. 2.
2. Harold Innis, *The Bias of Communication* (Toronto, 1951).
3. See James Clifford and George E. Marcus, eds., *Writing Culture. The Poetics and Politics of Ethnography* (Berkeley and Los Angeles, 1986), esp. Clifford's introduction, "Partial Truths," pp. 1–26.
4. Jack Goody, "Restricted Literacy in Northern Ghana," in *Literacy in Traditional Societies*, ed. Goody, pp. 201–2.
5. Cf. Clifford Geertz, "Thick Description: Toward an Interpretive Theory of Culture," in *The Interpretation of Cultures* (New York, 1973), p. 12.
6. Richard Rorty, *Philosophy and the Mirror of Nature* (Princeton, 1979).
7. "The Problem of Speech Genres," in M. M. Bakhtin, *Speech Genres and Other Late Essays*, trans. Vern W. McGee, ed. C. Emerson and M. Holquist (Austin, 1986), p. 60.
8. Werner Kelber, *The Oral and the Written Gospel* (Philadelphia, 1983).
9. *De Doctrina Christiana*, prooemium 8, *Corpus Christianorum Series Latina* vol. 32 (Turnhout, 1962), p. 5.
10. See ch. 1, pp. 22–24.
11. Roman Ingarden, *The Cognition of the Literary Work of Art*, trans. R. A. Crowley and K. R. Olson (Evanston, Ill., 1973), ch.4.
12. Hayden White, "The Value of Narrativity in the Representation of Reality," in *Content of the Form*, pp. 1–25.
13. See Erving Goffman, *Interaction Ritual* (New York, 1967) and *Relations in Public*.
14. Neusner, *Oral Torah*, p. xvi and passim. The following paragraph draws largely on this study.
15. Jacob Neusner, "The Bavli in Particular: Defining a Document in the Canon of Judaism in Relationship to the Old Testament," *Journal for the Study of the Old Testament* 33 (1985): 120. But see now also id., *The Formation of the Jewish Intellect* (Atlanta, 1988), which appeared too late to be considered here.
16. Wayne Meeks, *The First Urban Christians: The Social World of the Apostle Paul* (New Haven, 1983).
17. Ibid., p. 73.

CHAPTER EIGHT
Tradition and Modernity: Models from the Past

1. See S. N. Eisenstadt, *Post-Traditional Societies* (New York, 1972); id., *Tradition, Change, and Modernity* (New York, 1973); S. N. Eisenstadt and S. R. Graubard, eds., *Intellectuals and Tradition* (New York, 1973); Shils, *Tradition;* and J. C. Heesterman, *The Inner Conflict of Tradition: Essays in Indian Ritual, Kingship, and Society* (Chicago, 1985).

2. M.-D. Chenu, "Antiqui, moderni," *Revue des sciences philosophiques et théologiques* 17 (1928): 82–94; E. R. Curtius, *European Literature and the Latin Middle Ages,* trans. W. R. Trask (New York, 1963), pp. 251–55, 385, 484; Edouard Jeauneau, "'Nani gigantum humeris insidentes': Essai d'interprétation de Bernard de Chartres," in *Lectio Philosophorum: Recherches sur l'Ecole de Chartres* (Amsterdam, 1973), pp. 55–73; Hubert Silvestre, "'Quanto iuniores, tanto perspicaciores': Antécédents á la querelle des anciens et des modernes," in *Recueil commémoratif du Xᵉ anniversaire de la faculté de philosophie et lettres* (de Kinshasa), (Louvain, 1968), pp. 231–55; W. Hartmann, "'Modernus' und 'Antiquus': Zur Verbreitung und Bedeutung dieser Bezeichnungen in der wissenschaftlichen Literatur vom 9. bis zum 12. Jahrhundert," in *Antiqui et moderni: Traditionsbewusstsein und Fortschrittsbewusstsein im späten Mittelalter,* ed. A. Zimmermann (Berlin, 1974), pp. 21–39; and Elisabeth Gössmann, *Antiqui und Moderni im Mittelalter: Eine geschichtliche Standortsbestimmung* (Munich, 1974).

3. For a recent review of the issues, see above all *Renaissance and Renewal in the Twelfth Century,* ed. Benson and Constable.

4. For a recent example of the genre, distorting the work of some French and German scholars, see John Van Engen, "The Christian Middle Ages as an Historiographical Problem," *American Historical Review* 91 (1986): 519–52.

5. I am indebted to Martin Krygier for this summary of his, Edward Shils's, and Jerzy Szacki's central themes. Szacki's views are found in *Tradycja: Przegląd problematyki* (Warsaw, 1971), and are conveniently summarized by Krygier, "Tipologia della tradizione," *Intersezioni* 5 (1985): 221–49, and "Law as Tradition," *Law and Philosophy* 5 (1986): 237–62. For Shils's views, see his *Tradition.*

6. See *The Invention of Tradition,* ed. E. J. Hobsbawm and Terence Tanger (Cambridge, 1983).

7. See Jack Goody, *The Logic of Writing and the Organization of Society,* chs. 1 and 3, pp. 1–44, 87–126.

8. See Keith Michael Baker, "Memory and Practice: Politics and the Representation of the Past in Eighteenth-Century France," *Representations* 11 (1985): 134–64.

9. See the essays in *Writing Culture,* ed. Clifford and Marcus.

10. See James Duncan, *The City as Text: The Politics of Landscape Interpretation in the Kandian Kingdom* (Cambridge, 1990), and, for a broader survey, Deborah Winslow, "A Political Geography of Deities: Space and the Pantheon of Sinhalese Buddhism," *Journal of Asian Studies* 43 (1984): 273–91.

11. See Victor Turner, "Pilgrimages as Social Processes," in *Dramas, Fields, and Metaphors: Symbolic Action in Human Society* (Ithaca, N.Y., 1974), pp. 166–230.

12. Cf. Dean C. Tipps, "Modernization Theory and the Comparative Study of Societies: A Critical Perspective," *Comparative Studies in Society and History* 14 (1973): 205–16.

13. See Marion J. Levy, *Modernization and the Structure of Societies* (Princeton, 1966); Clifford Geertz, *Agricultural Involution: The Process of Ecological Change in Indonesia* (Berkeley and Los Angeles, 1966); and, more generally, Reinhard Bendix, "Tradition and Modernity Reconsidered," *Comparative Studies in Society and History* 9 (1967): 292–346.

14. See Gössman, *Antiqui und Moderni,* chs. 2–3, pp. 20–62.

15. See *Anticlaudianus,* ed. R. Bossuat (Paris, 1955), book 9, verses 380–409, pp. 196–97.

16. M. M. Bakhtin, *The Dialogic Imagination,* ed. Michael Holquist, trans. C. Emerson and M. Holquist (Austin, 1981), quoting respectively p. 16 and p. 15.

17. "Dialogus Duorum Monachorum," ed. R. B. C. Huygens, *Studi medievali,* 3d ser., 13 (1972): 375–470.

18. Heesterman, *Inner Conflict of Tradition,* p. 2.

INDEX